Running in rhythm with the heart

A book on the love of running, and the dream to cross the finish line of the longest race in the world – the 3100 Mile Race

Jayasalini Olga Abramovskikh
Running in rhythm with the heart

A book on the love of running, and the dream to cross the finish line of the longest race in the world – the 3100 Mile Race.

A love of running opens the doors to a new world of self-discovery. 3100 miles of self-transcendence.... the extreme conditions in this, the longest race in the world, help one to find the source of endless energy within.
Practical running and training advice blend harmoniously with inspiring stories. This book would be of interest to a wide variety of readers aiming for new goals and for self-discovery. This book is about having faith in dreams and taking steps towards their fulfillment.

Additional information: **loveofsports.org**

Contents

Dedication

I dedicate this book to the one who taught me to believe in myself, to believe in the power of the soul, and never to give up – my spiritual teacher Sri Chinmoy. By his own example he showed me how inner qualities such as strength, determination, love and faith can find an outer manifestation in each action, how sports can help along the self-perfection road and how aspiring for constant progress can become a means to be happy.

Sri Chinmoy is also the founder of the race that I will describe in this book – the longest certified race in the world, the 3100 Mile Race.

The fullness of life
Lies in dreaming and manifesting
The impossible dreams.
- Sri Chinmoy[1]

Introduction

Everybody has a dream in life, the dream that beckons like a distant star high in the sky. At first it may seem to be so far beyond reach that it is difficult even to call it a goal. Goals are situated a bit lower, somewhere at the level of the top of a tree or the roof of a building. To get there you have to work hard, climbing from one branch to another, sometimes overcoming the fear of falling down, but to reach the top of the tree or to climb the stairs of the building to get to the roof seems very realistic.

Each time you get higher and higher there is more faith that one day another treetop will be so close to the cherished dream-star that it would be possible to jump and reach it without fail. The bright light of that planet does not stop beckoning you because it is always inside your heart, even in those moments when you do not think of it consciously. It simply lives, it breathes and its heart beats. It has

---

1   Sri Chinmoy, Arise! Awake! Thoughts of a Yogi, Frederick Fell, Inc., 1972

9

unbelievable beauty. If you take a good look at it, it will take your breath away and everything becomes so clear and simple. There is only this goal and the rest is merely a series of steps paving the way to it.

I experienced such a dream quite unexpectedly when I was 25. It appeared in the period of my life when I had already understood that it was necessary to be brave in your aspirations, paying no attention to the sceptics around you. Running rushed into my life with the determination of a finishing sprinter. My speed at the time more resembled the unhurried movement of an ant, not even close by comparison to the speed of a flying butterfly, a racing hare or much less a running deer. I had just run my first marathon in the city of Miass around the pristine lake Turgoyak with my venerable 4 hours and 41 minutes. The happiness of self-transcendence that I felt at the finish could be compared only with listening to one's national anthem while standing on the podium of the Olympics. That day I felt that for me running was not the mechanical putting of one foot in front of the other, there was something magical in it....

Soon I met someone who had taken part in the longest race in the world – the 3100 Mile Race, held in New York City. I only vaguely remember what he told me that day. I had only one conscious feeling – I would run it. The feeling was so strong and distinct that in two months I applied for the race without any hesitation.

When you do not know what to expect, there is no fear – instead you have absolute certainty that everything will turn out well. Perhaps that is what they say about beginner's luck, that in reality the beginners are never afraid. I was ready to dive into an unknown ocean completely and without turning back, just feeling that its waters were calling me.

Two months after applying for the 3100 Mile Race I received the invitation to participate in a 10 day race instead. It upset me a bit. I thought ten days would be too short, and would pass too quickly. I wanted the experience of running and running, feeling there would be neither a beginning nor an end to it.

By that time I had been practicing regular meditation for about a year. The way I took any important decisions in my life was by listening to the inner voice – I tried to feel the guidance of my soul through meditation and to follow it. As soon as I had received the invitation for the 10 day race, I sat to meditate, the main thing I felt was gratitude for having such an opportunity. A feeling came that those multiday races offered a special service to the world, that they were not only necessary for the runners themselves, but also that the race was for everyone. I was very lucky that it was me who got the opportunity to run there and offer something special to the world, and now, three months prior to the race it was high time to get ready.

The training was intense; the race unbelievable. I was experiencing at the time something that had never happened to me before. And again I started dreaming about the 3100 Mile Race. Eight years went by. I ran seven multiday races, one per year, and the training became more and more extended. The running was complemented by cycling and

swimming. I wanted to develop not only in the direction of racing, but I also came to like many new things. I finished two Ironman triathlons with a PB of 11h 40 min, and swam across Zurich Lake – 26 km. However, the highest dream remained permanent. I simply waited. What for? I did not know exactly when, but I knew a moment would come when it would be clear the time was right.

In August of 2013 I happened to be at the spot where that historic race took place every year. At first I was walking, trying to enjoy the air of that place that was pulling me like a magnet. Then I ran. Suddenly, looking at the concrete surface, I felt as if I saw myself running there the next year. That moment I understood that very soon there would come a time when I would run there again, only as an official participant.

All that was so unusual – it was not the first time that I had visited the place, but I had never had such a feeling before. Days passed and the feeling became even more solid. Again and again I felt that the time was coming, and very soon I would run it....

In this book I would like to share the story of my experiences during the preparation and then participation in this longest-in-the-world certified race – the Self-Transcendence 3100 Mile Race. The Sri Chinmoy Marathon Team has been organizing it for over 20 years, yet less than 40 people have so far finished it. This is a dream that calls many ultramarathoners, the "Everest" of unparalleled height, the journey of unprecedented length.. It takes place every year in New York, during the hottest summer months. The runners need to cover

3100 miles in 52 days, running every day from 6 am until midnight. They average 60 miles per day (96 km) on an 800 meter sidewalk around a college and playgrounds – a tiny loop that opens unlimited horizons of new experiences. I sincerely hope this story will add at least a drop of inspiration and determination to the reader who has decided to follow their soul's voice and reach their Dream-Goal.

The aspiring heart has no fear...
The aspiring heart has a flame,
a burning, mounting flame
that mounts towards the Highest.
Where there is light, there cannot be fear.
- Sri Chinmoy[2]

TRAINING

Speed development

In the autumn before the race I presumed what the next year would be like for me. The spring promised to be full of long training, so I thought that the late autumn would be a time for building up my speed. Maintaining speed is always important to me. While doing long-distance running it is too easy to forget about speed training and engage fully in increasing mileage – something I often do. Hence from time to time I consciously remind myself of the necessity to develop and maintain speed.

Having rested after the summer season and already missing my running, I very gladly resumed

2   Sri Chinmoy, Earth's cry meets Heaven's smile, part 2, Agni Press, 1974

the training. At first I began incorporating speed intervals, at a moderate pace, into my training. Soon, having felt my body enter training mode, I introduced two days of short speed workouts per week. The training looked as follows:

1. Warm-up jogging for a mile

2. Stretching for about 10 minutes

3. Special running exercises – approximately 10 different exercises for 50 m plus two light accelerations at the end

4. Uphill speed work – 6 to 10 times per 150 m

5. Cooling down about a mile

In order to see my progress in speed development more distinctly, now and then I checked my time for a few distances: 100 m, 400 m and 1 km. I chose such short distances on purpose, as I wanted to remember what sprinting speed was about, to hear the swish of air in my ears and to feel the concentration of an arrow, when no thought was able to enter my mind while I ran. I had not trained at a stadium track for a long time and I was jumping with joy to run the curves. Speed training is not in the least like long runs of many hours. I very much enjoy both types of training, but speed always gives a bright feeling of joy, a burst of emotion and delight. For me a long distance means diving deep within, discovering poise and patience. This is a wonderful opportunity to open up my deepest capacities and to manifest reserves I have never imagined in myself.

The beginning of the New Year

The New Year always has something mysterious about it. We hope positive changes will come with it, that it will bring new inspiration. It is often said that as you meet the New Year so you will live it. I very much wanted to enter 2014 in a special way. I knew that my main objective for the year was to fulfil the dream of starting the race. Then an idea came to me: Why not meet the New Year with running.

I knew that in the city of Smolensk there were 24, 12 and 6-hour races. The moment I thought about it a wave of excitement ran through my body. It was like the feeling from childhood when you are looking for a miracle on New Year's night. Now I also felt that if I ran in the Smolensk night race surely something wonderful would happen and I would get to the start of the race in New York. Because of all those thoughts the anticipation of the night race was very exciting. I bought the train ticket and registered for the start. I wanted to run in Smolensk with my friend who had already agreed to be with me and to help me at the race in New York. Everything was working out perfectly. Later on, from time to time thoughts came – that I was not ready to run even 6 hours, that I had to go so far on New Year's Eve, and many more – but the determined promise to myself that I was going to run on New Year's Eve anyway helped a lot. The doubts went away.

At the race in Smolensk everything was beautiful and inspiring, and the finish of the 6-hour race did add confidence. There was a feeling inside that now I was bound to be at the 3100 Mile Race.

Having returned home I continued dreaming... and started planning my training.

Step by step

In January of 2014, when I was on vacation in Thailand, I liked running on a route by the sea. It was a rocky road going higher than the beach zone. The sea view opened only occasionally but the road was almost empty of cars so I was able to enjoy clean air, the singing of birds and beautiful blossoming trees along the way. Sometimes the blossoms fell down on the asphalt and I picked them up and ran for some time with a flower in my hand – I liked it enormously. The road was marked by a great deal of hills. It often went uphill so that a hilltop was unseen behind the turn. When I ran it the first time I did not expect to see so many hills. Right in the middle of the first one, not seeing the end of the rise, I switched to walking. Getting to the top I saw that the hill ended almost immediately after the turn and there was a nice downhill. I studied the area; it was indeed very hilly. Slopes were followed by rises with a few flat spots. However, now I knew that the steep part of even the longest rise was not more than 200 m, and after that it got easier. During my first run on that route I switched to walking many times, but I dearly wanted to be able to cover the whole route

nonstop. The goal was aflame inside me.

Next day, when I ran up the first and longest hill, I decided not to look up, but to focus on the tiles under my feet. All I had to do was to pass over one square tile after another. I had a simple task – to run one square after another. I did not think about the long steep rise anymore. I had only the squares in front of me, and the simple task of moving forward. The tile design flew past my eyes. I only put my foot on the next tile. Having concentrated on this specific task, I thought about the physical hardship of it considerably less. To my great surprise I found myself close to the turn that meant the end of the rise in some ten meters. Getting to the top I noticed that my quads were nearly burning but I resolutely continued my running. The feeling would pass in some twenty meters. In that way all the remaining hills went by and I managed to run to the end of the road without stops. Then I joyfully jumped into the sea and enjoyed a well-deserved swim. The goal was reached. Yet could I become so well trained overnight? The day before I had stopped at each rise but today I was able to run all the hills. Could that have been merely the fear of the mind yesterday and not the tiredness of muscles?

Immediately I thought that during the summer race it would be best to think only of the next step, never trying to envision even the end of one day, definitely not to think of the following day, and not to count the days remaining until the finish.

Meeting Suprabha

In January I was lucky to meet Suprabha, the runner from Washington who had finished the distance of 3100 miles more than anyone else on earth (13 times, as of the beginning of 2015). Moreover, she had finished the distance of 2700 miles, the race preceding the 3100 Mile Race.

When we were talking about training she remembered the words of Sri Chinmoy, the founder of the race, on the importance of extensive training days when you run a distance exceeding the marathon. First of all, it is important to get rid of the fear of distance. Runners, like any other people, may have doubts about whether they are able to do what they have never done. However, when in training, one repeatedly runs distances exceeding the marathon and does it for a few days in a row. One gets confidence and the mind stops being afraid of long distances. At the same time, during this type of long distance training, the body remembers the capacity to run for a long time even with the feeling of tiredness. The marathon distance is like the top of the mountain – having surmounted it many times you are no longer afraid of a new height.

Furthermore, Suprabha told me a lot about the necessity of good nutrition with the consumption of considerable amounts of calories, and about coming to the race with some extra weight to help avoid losing too many kilograms in the first two weeks of the race. She recommended taking a lot of fats at the race, such as coconut oil or ghee (clarified butter), with some added honey.

She also mentioned salt balance and the drink she had used – water with salt, sugar or honey and some lemon juice or any other juice.

Training schedule

Based on my experience I started distance training for a multiday race three months before the start. So it happened that time, too. In January I ran for six hours straight. It was rather relaxed running, resulting in something over 60 km. After that I started running for an hour a few times per week.

I decided to follow the advice on distance training and tried to fill my weekend with long distance running – often it was 50-60 km each day. Here are my running totals by months:

February	March	April	May
406 km	567 km	585 km	462 km

March and April became the most intensive training months of my life. It seemed I had never run so much. Below I give the detailed table of the training schedule by week for each month. On other days the distance was approximately 8-15 km.

Week #	February	March	April	May
1		60 + 20	60 + 52	60 + 51
2	42 + 58	19+24+ 6 0 + 5 2 +42	60 + 30	30+30+ 1 0 + 3 0 +30
3		20 + 20	52	63 + 63
4	42 + 25	60 + 52	35 + 60	50 + 25
Rest days, total	3	9	4	10

All the main days of the training schedule were in the cool season. Normally I went out for a run at 6 or 7 am, taking along some hot tea, a few bananas and dates, which I left in my car, and started running. The circle of asphalted streets in my village was a weaving route with many light slopes and rises, skirting the pond, passing a railroad station and continuing onto the main street of the village. There were very different houses on both sides of the road – small and old-style cottages with pensioners living in them for their entire life, and new huge modern houses with owners of nearly cosmic automobiles. Along the way there were a few village water pumps and even a well. Some locals still get water there. When it got hot I also stopped occasionally to enjoy a drink of cold well water.

The surface of my training road was asphalted, which was an advantage. The race organizers' advice was to get used to hard surfaces before the race, as it would help to avoid injuries on the unusually hard concrete surface of the race course.

The route that I ran was of a shuttle type. It

ended at the barred gate of a guarded village, with a booth for the guards. On reaching the booth I turned and ran back. The guards could not help noticing my frequent and unusually long runs. They always greeted me and asked what round I was on and how many were left. They often wanted to talk to me – why and for what I had been running for so long, how it was possible, plus a thousand more questions. Sometimes I stopped for 5 to 10 minutes and told them about my training plan. We eagerly discussed amazing achievements in sports, or simply the weather forecast. Even when it was impossible to communicate we made sure to give a cheery wave.

I checked the time of my long runs. I wanted to run not only for a long time but also at a certain tempo – that was why I could not chat for too long.

In those 3 to 4 months of regular running I made friends with a lot of locals. Some of them were simply greeting me; others jokingly asked every time, "Why are you running so far again?" When spring came and the trees turned green, one of the neighbors insistently suggested I channel my energy into cutting the branches of trees instead – he was dead sure it was more useful. In reply I always laughed and asked if he would like to start running. Then we laughed loudly and went on with our respective occupations – gardening and running.

One circuit of the village was about 9.5 km but I found a way to round it up to 10 – it was easier to count that way. At one straight line I turned and did two laps – in this way I could gain an additional 500 meters to make 10 km per lap. The first 20 km I always ran without eating or drinking, then at each round I came up to the car, poured myself a mug of hot tea and took something to eat – as a rule it was a banana or some dates which I ate on the go.

It turned out that the classic marathon distance was indeed a magical number. After 40-45 km something inexplicable started happening to my body, and it was difficult to maintain the previous speed. I noticed that after the marathon distance it took me a few minutes more to run one round, sometimes it was up to 3-5 minutes more. My long training was getting long indeed. I was preparing myself for something I had never done; therefore my training was also longer than I had ever done.

On weekdays, when I ran 8-15 km I made sure to add some exercises. I skipped uphill on one foot or on both feet, did side strides, ran backwards. As a rule, I did every exercise for 50 m each leg. On the circuit I had 3-4 long slopes where I did these exercises.

Beside that, after finishing I did some light stretching in the yard, walking on the inner and outer sides of my feet, on the heels and toes, and strengthening my feet by rising on my toes on the steps of a staircase.

My entire day was dedicated to preparation. While waiting for a suburban electric train, again I raised on my feet to strengthen them. At work, while going somewhere, I managed to do some light stretching and during my lunch break I went to a sauna to get used to the heat. When I went up the escalator of the underground, I put my feet on the steps in such a way that my heels remained in the air, thus helping to stretch the heel tendons. I felt

that even the simplest exercises and unelaborate means of preparation were important, and the accumulated effect would provide some result.

I also felt that it was important to be conscious during the training – that is, while doing an exercise, running or even going upstairs I tried to feel that every movement made me stronger, more robust and more suited to endurance.

It is possible to do the same exercises while remaining in your thoughts at work, with friends, in a bed with a cup of hot chocolate, and then the effect of training will be quite different. We get stronger not only from what we do, but also from why we do it, and it is awareness in action that brings about long-awaited training effects. Going up a long escalator, I knew it was excellent training for my legs. Yet if I simply rushed upstairs because I wanted to catch the last train, the training effect would be quite different.

Adaptation to extreme temperatures

Once in November of 2013, when I was on the electric train on my way to work, I saw a sportsman sitting on the opposite side. Whereas everybody was wearing winter jackets, he had just sports shorts and a T-shirt on. I thought that was quite unusual, but I was not overly surprised, as I had already seen people who would not wear anything warmer than a shirt or a jersey in winter. For some reason he was also looking at me attentively and then asked if I was a runner. At my positive answer he exclaimed that he had seen a documentary about me, produced by TV-channel Russia 2 – *Adventures of the Body, Extra-endurance Test*. So we spoke about ultra-long distances and of course I could not help showing interest in his clothing. He told me that a year ago he had decided to try to condition himself to the cold and gradually he stayed out longer with a minimum of clothes on, ran in shorts and T-shirt in any season and in any weather. All that resulted in his not having any colds since then.

That entire story impressed me quite a lot. I thought since there were many people easily enduring the cold, not using warm clothes even at minus 30 degrees centigrade and staying healthy, I would also be able to do that. After all, I also had two arms, two legs and one head like them. So what was wrong with me? For me that was truly intriguing. I decided that I must try it.

Not wanting to delay the experiment, in a few days when the temperature was at a stable minus 7 degrees centigrade, I put on a cotton T-shirt, long but thin leggings, gloves and a cap. It seemed to me that cotton would warm me better.

During such experiments the most important things are your mood, emotions and thoughts. It is important never to allow the slightest hesitation, not even one negative thought even for a fraction of a second.

Before going out I sincerely prayed for the higher forces to stay with me and follow each of my steps. Then I warmed up in the entrance hall, making a few circular moves with my hands, inhaled deeply, and plucking up my courage, opened the street door. Without the least possible doubt or fear I ran out at once rather quickly. The stars brightly shone in the sky like a thousand flashlights. There were pure white snowdrifts everywhere – the entire picture gave an unbelievable thrill and absolutely indescribable feelings. I was literally overflowing with emotions from all of that. I could not believe it, but indeed the cold was not to be felt. I ran and was almost jumping up in the air with a puppy's delight. It all seemed completely unreal. After about a kilometer I started to feel how powerfully my blood was circulating through my entire body, especially in my arms. I ran rather quickly and felt the wind on my skin. Even the smell of frosty air became brighter and juicier and I was overwhelmed with joy from it. The entire distance of my first conditioning-to-the-cold run was about three kilometers. I decided not to push too hard. Getting home I thanked the universe for that experience and promptly took a hot shower. I felt like a real superhero and decided that I would continue with the practice.

Later I gradually increased my T-shirt runs up to 50 minutes. Something told me that the ability of the body to adapt to changes in temperature, even cold ones, may help me at the race with high temperatures. Perhaps the idea of conditioning oneself to the cold while training for a race in the heat looks strange, but later I felt that it really helped me, both emotionally and physically.

Beside that, I started to visit a dry sauna for the balance of temperatures, and to get more focused on the adaptation of the body to high temperatures. I came to know that many runners preparing for a desert race use the sauna, gradually prolonging their stay in it and even doing some easy exercises. The middle temperature in the sauna at my sports club was about 85-90 degrees centigrade. At first I could stay there no longer than 10-12 minutes, but gradually 15-17 minutes became the norm, and did not cause discomfort. The next step was doing some easy exercises. I tried to do some slight twists of the body and some leg raises, bending and straightening the knees. It turned out that at the beginning, even with those simple exercises, it was much more difficult to stay inside for the full 15 minutes. With great interest I observed how easily the body adapted and got used to any conditions. Even in 10-14 days it is possible to perform things that present difficulties in the beginning. Later at the race I learned that William, the runner from Scotland, also used a sauna in his training.

Incidents before the race

I have noticed many times that before a significant event some quite unexpected incidents

occur. It looks like a test of determination, a readiness to overcome all difficulties on the way to the goal, or even on the way to the commencement of realizing that goal. That start was not an exception either – moreover, it was a serious challenge, a test of my ability to surmount all upcoming obstacles and, most importantly, of my ability not to allow a shadow of a doubt to settle inside. Here I will tell of only a few incidents.

Once, when I was already finishing a long run, having more than 50 kilometers behind me, I left the main asphalted road and continued running on the roadside. Suddenly I nearly fell down, due to an acute stabbing pain in my right foot. What was that? Almost at once I realised that I had stepped on something sharp. Lifting my foot I saw a huge rusty nail sticking out from the sole of my running shoe. I burst into tears – the nail was really huge. I got it out despite unbelievable pain and pulled my shoe off to inspect the wound. Already the sock was crimson with blood, so I did not even try to see any more and simply hopped on one leg to the road, to wait for a passing car. Within a few minutes a car stopped, and the driver told me that he had seen me many times during my training. When he saw me hitching a lift he realised that something had happened. He helped me and I was able to get home. Then I called my good friend, who was a doctor, and asked her what to do. She insistently recommended that I go to a hospital and later I saw it was very good advice. There they removed a piece of rust from the wound, keeping it from unnecessary inflammation later on. They also gave me an injection against tetanus. One might say I got away with only a slight fright: a few days without running, two dressings in the hospital, then attending to the wound by myself and being able to return to running in a few days.

The next story is connected with my tendency to constantly invent something new for my training. I started to think about possible improvements to the training process. I really wanted to try new things and arrive at a higher performance level. Then I got the idea to improve my flexibility, as I never was noted for my suppleness. I was sure that with better stretching I would be able to run faster and recover in a shorter period of time. It would help me to withstand the strain.

So I began to attend a stretching class and to pay more attention to stretching. I liked it a lot and I felt the effects. The days when I had a good stretch after my long runs, my recovery was much faster and I was able to run the next day at the same speed for 5 hours. Without stretching, my speed on the next day of long running was considerably lower as a rule.

I saw evident progress in my stretching but I wanted to intensify the process even more, so I chose an instructor from my sports club. She conducted the class and I told her about my goal, so she started to work with me individually. Our first meeting was at the beginning of May, during the holidays. On the morning of that day I had run for more than 5 hours, then I took a shower and went to the club. The training was excellent – I started to imagine how I would be even more flexible in two weeks and the back surfaces of my hips would at last give in to stretching. After that training, the next day I ran again, as if I had not had a long training run the day before. In a few days we met again and all was fine – I was surprised how supple my body and muscles became. One of the exercises was the setting of the legs wide apart with a deep bending forward. I bent smoothly more and more, one centimeter after another. A few minutes passed but we went on stretching in that position. Suddenly I heard some sound coming from the back part of my hip, right under the gluteal muscles. I grew apprehensive but decided that the phenomenon was natural. I straightened up for a moment and then proceeded with the stretching for a minute more. After the class was over, I found that it was difficult to walk. With difficulty I went to work, and for a few days I could not even dream about running. The start of the race was less than a month away. I was totally bewildered.

In a few days I tried to run but it was awkward and lame running. The back of my hip was tense and stretching was out of the question. Consequently I had to go to the race with an injured hip, and the first half of the race I often used an elastic bandage to support and stabilize the muscles.

Experiments before an important start turned out not to be the best of ideas. It is more sensible not to try new ways of training in the last month. It is better to try out any new methods beforehand and prior to the start use only those you are sure of – some tried-and-tested training with a well-known effect.

Nevertheless, I knew for sure that I would appear at the start of the race without fail – despite all the incidents. Even for a fraction of a second I did not allow the thought of not running it.

When a dream is formed
Inside the mind,
It may never be manifested.
But when a dream is blossomed
Inside the heart,
It is bound to be manifested
Either today, or in the near future.

- Sri Chinmoy[3]

THE RACE

New York, New York

We landed in an already familiar airport and border control asked me about the purpose of my visit. I had to say what kind of competition awaited me. A slightly surprised officer asked to see my invitation and, having read it, said that he was also a runner and was getting ready for a marathon. He smiled and wished me good luck.

On arriving in New York my helper Pati and I stayed at the house of our friend, an amiable and cheerful girl, Lyalya. The house was located not far from the race course, which was very convenient. I was very happy for the opportunity to stay there. I

---

3   Sri Chinmoy, Twenty-Seven Thousand Aspiration-Plants, part 239, Agni Press, 1997

had a private room with a shower close by, and Pati stayed in the adjacent room. The house was very cosy and beautiful. I started calling it home at once and it did become my true home, where I would long to get to each night. The only thing we were worrying about before the race was a high and long staircase. To get to the room I had to climb more than twenty steep steps leading to the second floor. My helpers Manjaree and Pati were a bit concerned whether or not I would be able to do it every day – going downstairs in the morning and upstairs in the evening. Sandhani, one of the race directors, upon hearing our worries laughed and said that Suprabha had climbed 21 steps every day of her 13 years of participation. After that we relaxed and decided that I, too, would be able to deal with the stairs.

When I went to bed the first night, I could not wait for the next morning: I knew that I would rush to the race course.

Establishing a connection with the course before the start

After waking up the next day at 5 am I decided without any hesitation that it was the best time to go to the race course. It was already quite light outside. I had had a plan of what I wanted to do at

the course.

I have observed many times how sportspeople perform their ceremonial at the Olympics and other big competitions. They say their special words and make certain gestures that help and give them faith – in their luck and in higher forces near them. I also wanted to come to the course and do what would give me additional faith. It was especially symbolic for me.

Having finished my ceremonial, I decided to run a few laps as a warm-up, plus I wanted to feel something – I did not even know what I had to feel but was sure that after waiting so long for that moment some feelings might come.

Soon I saw some people running towards me. Who could they be? In fact it was two of the other runners, Vasu and Teekshanam. I noticed a plastic bag in Vasu's hands. He told me that every time before the start he collected all the trash along the course. It helped him to establish an inner connection with this place and to do something good for the course. He said that the course withstood thousands of blows from our feet but nonetheless helped us throughout 50 days, and the course trees shaded us from the burning sun with their branches. In turn he very much wanted to do something good for the course. So it turned out that everybody had a personal ritual before the start.

Later on, during the race, many a time I saw Vasu picking up chocolate wrappers and other trash. He said it was doubly useful – the course became cleaner and by removing garbage he removed obstacles, plus the bending helped to stretch the back and it was a good way to squat.

Interestingly, I have never thought that for the earth we walk and run on, it may not be easy to withstand all our steps, and it might even be painful for her.

The idea of cleaning the course echoed in my heart and the next morning, when we accidentally met again, each of us had a bag in our hands.

Briefing before the start

Two days prior to the start the organizers had a briefing for runners, telling us many things about the technical side of the race and a few important moments – basically for those running for the first time. For 3 out of 14 runners all that was happening around them was new, and I was amongst those lucky ones. It was an interesting team – participants from Eastern and Western Europe, Ukraine, Russia, Australia, Scotland, and America. The youngest ones were Sopan from Bulgaria and I – we were both 33. Sopan had finished for the first time 11 years before, when he was 22, and became the youngest finisher. The oldest participant was 60-year-old William from Scotland, who would try to be the first 'over 60' man finishing in the race. Was it possible at 60? William looked much younger than his age, fresh

and merry, not tall, but slim and lean. You could feel the strength in him and the high functioning of his muscles. Another senior participant was 59-year-old Ray from America, who had an unbelievable number of multiday races behind him – more than 30. In his youth he had not only been suited to endurance, but was also very fast – a completely unorthodox person, to whom I would like to dedicate a chapter later in the book.

We were told that four participants would be brought to the race every morning by car and every evening taken home. The others got bikes, and would come and go by themselves. In general, the privilege to go by car was passed to the girls. At first I even wanted to ask for a bike and decline the car – I imagined with what pleasure I would go by bike early in the morning, feeling flows of fresh morning air on my face. Then I remembered Suprabha's advice on the convenience of going by car, especially when it was raining, plus you need to bring a lot of stuff – running shoes, clothes, some additional equipment. In short, I decided not to create additional difficulties. Since the girls were offered rides, I would rather agree, and so I did.

Three representatives of the medical team told us about the importance of hydration – that it was necessary to drink a lot, but not only water, preferably isotonic and other drinks as well, to help maintain salt and mineral balance. One of the popular drinks was coconut water. Also, one can add some salt, sugar and lemon to water, eat some seaweed, lick the finger after dipping it in a salt cellar – many quite different ways to care for your salt balance. One of the ways to check on your hydration is to pinch yourself on the back of your palm and observe how the skin reacts. If it remains lifted and takes up to a few seconds to flatten – that is to say does not go back at once – it is the first sign of dehydration. I could not believe that the skin would remain lifted, but during the race I witnessed that personally.

They also told us about the necessity of using sunblock, even if you did not feel like it. Thermal burn is a stress for the body. It has to spend additional energy to fight against one more inauspicious influence, so it is much wiser to avoid it and save some strength. Later on I found a wonderful spray for children with a protective factor of 50 SPF at a drugstore. The spray was more pleasant for the skin and I applied it four times a day – it was enough. The spray helped a lot. It was barely felt on the skin and protected just fine. Looking at my pale face it was difficult to believe that I was running day after day under the sun and at plus 30 degrees centigrade.

At the end of the briefing they took a picture of all the runners, helpers, organizers, cooks and medical staff. The most interesting things would start happening the following day – anticipation and light excitement were hanging in the air.

The evening after the briefing we had a pre-race dinner at the vegetarian restaurant Annam Brahma. There I first met Nidhruvi, another girl in the race. When she appeared with her helpers, she came up to me, put her hand on my shoulder and started laughing loudly – I laughed back. Our first meeting was very light and joyful.

At the end of the meeting William said he remembered me from the days of the 10 and 6-day race two years ago, where I had run 10 days and he had done 6. Then we spoke just a few phrases to each other. I remembered him at once, too – I recalled his amusing style of running with very little steps. He said that he had deliberately worked out that technique, and as he learned to run in small steps he ceased to get any injuries.

In the eyes of those running for the first time one could see some excitement. It was impossible even to imagine *what* would be happening over the next two months. It gave me shivers even to think of what would start tomorrow. Outwardly everybody was smiling and appeared to be at peace; nevertheless I could tell that my knees were shaking.

One day before the start

Reality like a dream

The first morning the car was at the entrance of our house earlier than usual, at 5:20, as we had to arrange all our things at the race, to sort out our running shoes and get in the mood for the race. A few TV reporters arrived, but all that was going on around did not resemble the 100 m start at the Olympics when the cheering crowd exulted with fervour. Here you got the distinct feeling of a home-like atmosphere.

The organizers invited the participants to the starting line one by one, where they introduced the runners, beginning with the newcomers. The last ones were those who had come a number of times and were amongst the winners. When all of us lined up I could not comprehend whether all that was happening was a dream or reality. But I did not have time to think about it too long, as Sahishnu, one of the race directors, began his pre-start speech. He said that it was much better for runners not to think about the finish line or to count remaining laps, but to remain in the present second, to think that despite all the difficulties it was such an honour to take part in this race. After this address we had a few moments of total silence. I think in those moments everybody was concentrating on to what or whom they dedicated the race. A minute-lasting eternity filled the space with colossal energy. This time there was no excitement – rather, all was full of peace and inner determination.

The first two circles we all ran together as one group – it was very symbolic, because during the

whole race the spirit of oneness continued to unite all the runners. Sincere mutual aid and genuine friendship literally permeated the air from the first moments. The first hour was followed by the second, and then by the third – everybody was running with much ease, nobody was in a hurry. I felt wonderful – having already run more than a marathon, I did not feel it, as the speed was not at all high.

Presently Vasu from St. Petersburg ran by me and asked, "Are you doing squats?" The question sounded rather strange to me.

"Do I have to?"

"Sure. Each few laps do a squat," was his answer.

From the very beginning I decided that I would observe and listen to those who had already run the 3100 a few times. Vasu's expertise was unquestionable, as he had finished first the previous year, plus he always helps everybody around him, just because his heart always wants to help his neighbour.

In short, I chose a spot where I would not be in the way of the others and did a squat. Instantly I understood why that was needed. I thought I would not feel any tightness in the muscles – it was only 5 hours of running, next to nothing. However all of the frontal part of the hips felt as though it had been 12 hours of running at a good tempo. I got up and continued running. The blood circulation in my muscles was clearly better. When I am keen on something, I go for it completely. The same went for the squats. I did one every two circles and in an hour felt the effect – soon I was able to do it quickly and easily. Sure enough, this eagerness for squats did not last long. I had to work out an optimal schedule of stretching, one that would be sufficiently effective but not too frequent and of course, not take too much time.

First lap

Stretching routine

Каждое утро на трассе я начинала с растяжки стопEach morning on the course I started by stretching my feet and shins. I hoped it would help to avoid shin splints.

Then the running day began. To run the entire day... what was it like, with what to compare it? To get some idea of how long it took I compared it

to my working day in the office. Every day I spend 9 hours at the computer, communicating with my colleagues, and it seems that my work lasts almost all day. At the race 9 hours marks exactly half a day. The running starts at 6 am so after 9 hours it is 3 pm, the time when I finish my first break and go to the course to begin the second part of the day. At the office after 9 hours you can go home, but here it is only one half of the day. This comparison always puts me into a state of incomprehension of what actually happened during the race – how everything that took place in the race was even possible... it had no comparison with my day-to-day life outside the race... spending 9 hours in the office, while during the race that was just half a day.

In the first days of the race it was psychologically difficult for me to be on the course for so long, to run without breaks. Then I invented periodic stretching for myself – first of all, it was a good excuse to switch to something different, to change the activity and the monotony of movement. Besides, it was quite a useful occupation, as it helped the muscles to recover. They stayed in much better tone and were less prone to tightness.

On the third or the fourth day I began to experiment. First I tried stretching every ten laps (one lap was about 800 m). In those 5-7 minutes that I gave to such stops, I managed to stretch the back and front parts of the hips and to stretch my spine and feet. All that happened rather quickly, but gave sufficient opportunity to ease the mind and body. I called those breaks "long ones".

On one of the first days I was running half a

lap with Pranjal, a participant from Slovakia. I told him that I had invented periodic stretches that I did every 10 laps, and that I would like to add some short intermediate ones every 5 laps. He smiled in reply, encouraged me and said that it was a nice idea. Later I understood how laughable the idea might have seemed to a person who never stopped for any stretching whatsoever. Pranjal always ran and did not spend a second on anything unnecessary, including massage and stretching. By the end of the race he began occasionally to shake his calves – the only thing he ever did with his legs – and I never saw him doing any warm-up or stretching.

However, I very much liked the idea of adding some short stretching, even though these two-minute stops lasted only a few days. Later I decided to start saving time and to have a more conscious attitude to each minute. Gradually I began to value more and more not only minutes, but also seconds. Meanwhile the duration and periodic pauses for stretching shortened. In the middle of the race there was one stretching session in the daytime and one in the evening. By the end of the race I had to switch on "the rigid economy" mode and get by with one session every 2-3 days.

Perhaps it was one of the reasons why my speed got slower by the end of the race – probably it is a good field for experimentation and I have yet to find my optimal ratio of pauses and running. However, that is for the next time.

Stretching before the start of a day

Getting acquainted with the shin

The first week was behind me. I enjoyed easy running and there was a feeling like sliding on perfect ice. The movement is unbelievably fast but you do not have to apply any effort, as the movement comes by itself, very easily and naturally. That day during the daytime break I got a massage from Hilary.

When she came I liked to get onto the massage table and while I was pulling off my leggings and stretching, to ask her how she was or to tell her the news from the course. I did like the process of communication, and I called the days when Hilary gave me a massage "happy days".

The first day a masseuse was expected, it was Hilary's turn. I liked the massage, and after a 25-minute break I ran further. In reality, we did not run further for the movement was always around the same circle, but for myself I clearly felt the forward movement. Most likely it was a feeling of progress to which every runner aspired – first of all, changing oneself as a person. It is difficult to say how it happens during running – probably when one overcomes all the difficulties one's attitude to life alters. All emotions, feelings, experiences become unbelievably keen, sincere and profound. There comes a clear feeling of what is important and really needed in life, and what is a mere trifle. In such moments you breathe your chest full and the words "to be an absolutely happy person" become a living reality.

That day I soared on wings of joy and lightness, there was an emerging feeling of certainty that everything was going to be fine, when in one moment I felt discomfort in my ankle. It was a sensation as if a bone was not in its place. I tried to do circular motions with my feet in the hope that everything would fit into place, but the discomfort did not go away – on the contrary it was turning into pain. Then I felt that if I neglected it the ankle would soon start to swell. I went up to Sahishnu, one of the race directors, and explained the problem – I was absolutely sure that a specialist would simply put the ankle right, but Sahishnu said that night he

was not able to call for any specialist. I continued to run, and observed how my leg began to swell and became more and more painful. It is an interesting state when you know you have to do something but do not understand what to do. By the evening the picture became clean and clear – it was a classic shin splint. By that time I was able only to walk – running was out of the question. One lap I met Nidhruvi, the runner from Austria. She asked what had happened to me and offered her help as readily and in as friendly a way as usual. Upon hearing my story she gave some advice on what I had to do at that moment, without delay. Later on, based on what Nidhruvi and other runners had recommended, I worked out an algorithm of what to do for shin splints and the overstrain of the lower legs:

- First of all to react to the first signs of inflammation: discomfort, light pain, limitation in flexibility of the ankle-joint etc.

- Check if anything is too tight at the discomfort zone – loosen the laces of the shoes, put the tongue right, try another pair of shoes.

- Start stretching the ankle joint and the calf muscles. Some variations of such stretching are shown in the pictures below.

There is an opinion that in order to get rid of shin splints it is necessary to act upon the front muscles of the lower leg and on the calves, as both of those groups of muscles influence the foot. At the race I chose a spot at the course and stopped every two laps for a few seconds to do the necessary exercises.

A. Stretching of calf's upper part

B. Stretching of calf's lower part and heel tendon

C. Stretching of ankle-joint tendon

First of all, I leaned against a tree or a pole and stretched the calf muscles, and after that I put my weight on the forefoot and stretched the arch. It is important to do it frequently, especially when the problem is just appearing. As the condition improves, the frequency can be decreased.

Below are listed some measures that I used for treating inflammation and overstraining in the area of the ankle joint:

- Under the forefoot, put a rolled out cabbage leaf (use a rolling-pin). The leaf must be rolled out so it gets soft and thin, and is leaking juice. Leave the

leaf under the forefoot while running.

- Put some ice on the arch during breaks.

- Fix the ankle joint with tape in order to reduce the looseness of the feet. You can use regular tape or kinesiology tape to fix the ankle joint at the circumference and to increase the inflow of lymph to the required area. I even saw how the runners fixed tape to the lacing of the running shoes in order to reduce the tension on the ankle muscles while raising the foot off the ground.

- Take preparations to help reduce the inflammation.

That night Nidhruvi's helper helped me to fix my feet with tape and I tried to run. My attempts to run were not successful, so I had to walk. Soon walking became so painful that I walked the circle in almost 20 minutes instead of the usual 9. Sandhani, who was riding his bike around the course every evening, asked me if I wanted to go home early and have a good night's sleep. It was 11 pm and I had completed 102 laps for the day. I considered it to be the best decision and just there, in the middle of the lap, asked Sandhani to inform my helper that we were going home. When I finished the lap we got into the car and in 7 minutes were home.

Walking upstairs 20 steps, as usual I stopped at the broad step in the middle. That's where every evening I stretched my feet, heel tendons and calves.

That time everything was more sensitive and even painful. After a shower I took a foot-bath with salt and baking soda, plus sometimes we added some hydrogen peroxide. The container was rather big, so the water covered half my calves. What bliss it was to put my feet into the warm salty water. Before going to sleep we cooled the inflamed area of the shin with ice, and Pati gave me a massage with all the creams we had. During an active massage with rather strong pressure, all the stagnant effects from the inflamed part of the shin were removed. I went to sleep with a sincere prayer for the healing of all my pain and the disappearance of the inflammation.

At the race I became convinced by my own experience that every sincere prayer is bound to be heard and fulfilled. Now, surely somebody would say: Not every one of them. But how many of our prayers are really sincere? At the race I knew that everything happening around me was unconditional Grace, and however hard I trained before the race, my physical body alone was not able to endure such pressure. Often an image came to me that I was on somebody's big and tender palms, and that they were carrying me day after day, lap after lap.

Awakening next morning at 5 am, I first of all made a circular motion with my ankle. With all my heart I hoped that I would not feel any pain, but in reply I got a sharp, acute pain, like lightning. In order not to get upset, I had to remember that before the start of the race I had decided to gladly receive every experience, whatever it would be. If difficulties come, it means I have the strength to overcome them. This thought cheered me up a lot, and I was able to accept the thought that I would probably be walking for the entire day. Nevertheless, before leaving, I asked all the higher forces to run in and

through me, as I myself was not at all able to do so. There was no sorrow inside me, no pain, no sadness – I was really ready to go through any experience and try to do that with the maximum joy. After lining up with all the participants on the starting line and after the 'Go.' command, I began to walk along the course. For a few circles I just walked. Then I thought that I had not even tried to run. Maybe I would be able to. After the first attempt I realized that I could run, although it was painful, and also I could alternate walking with running. Each circle I stretched and continued both to walk and to run. All my attention was focused on what was going on inside me and on the sensations in my leg. Near noon I felt that I did not have to be afraid, that I could try to run as before. Then I switched to walking only when the route briefly went uphill, and the rest of the time I ran.

I could run again. It was true happiness indeed. An unbelievable feeling, it was really fantastic. I could run again. The shin splints were over in half a day. From the point of view of physiology it is practically impossible; it can happen only due to Grace from above. This phrase can easily be applied to the whole of the race, to every second of those 52 days, to each meter of those 5000 kilometers. That day I ran the required 109 laps – I was able to build up some speed in the second half of the day. I ran and my heart was overflowing with gratitude: I knew everything that was happening was practically impossible to explain, but instead it was possible to experience and feel with every cell of my body.

That incident did not happen by chance. From the very beginning of the race until that day I had run the entire course, never switching to walking even when the route went uphill, as did the other runners. Surely I had noticed that the experienced participants walked up the inclines. They had some running sections and walking sections but I did not want to waste time on walking and ran the whole lap, walking only past the base camp near my helpers. I decided that, as I had done a lot of uphill running during my training at home, I was in good shape for that and could manage uphills there, too. Now I understand that it was far wiser to rely on the experience of those who had run the race many times. After that incident I decided to listen to the voice of reason and changed my strategy in relation to the uphill parts.

The daily routine

On the eve of the race, during the pre-race dinner, Nidhruvi asked me at what time I was going to take breaks. Sure enough, I was not able to answer specifically, as I had never tried races with a schedule where you run in the daytime and must rest at night. We decided that I would have breaks after Nidhruvi, which meant for me the first break at 1 pm and the second at 7 pm. At the beginning of the race each break lasted for 25-30 minutes. During that time I could have a massage, rest a bit, and I

could sleep for 5 minutes or so. My helpers changed the tape on my feet, then I put my socks and running shoes on and off I went.

After some time, I noticed that at approximately 1 pm a new amazing flow of energy came to me, and then the running became very easy. At that time there was maximum solar activity, and if I kept running with it until the break, after the break there was not so much time left with the sun – after 4 pm the sun was considerably less scorching. Also I noticed that in the mornings I had much more strength and energy. It always took me three laps to get into the running flow, since in the mornings my body was very stiff, but after that I could usually run quite effortlessly all the way until afternoon.

Since it was considerably easier to run in the morning than during the day, I tried to prolong the period before the first break and to shorten the last part before going home at night. Thus I arrived at an ideal schedule for myself, when the first break must be over by 3 pm, which is exactly one half of the day – that is, I had to have completed half of the required miles by that time. I always aimed for 55 laps by 3 pm. If I planned a 25-minute break, I left the course at 2:30, as I often stayed in the wagon a bit longer. It is surprising how time flies when you are resting.

The duration of the first break always depended on how many miles I had been able to run in the morning, and according to necessity, the rest time was sometimes shortened. In the first weeks it was comparatively easily for me to acquire the necessary half of the required laps – 55. By 2 pm I had them at my disposal, which meant that the additional miles before the break became a bonus. In the following weeks those 55 laps were done only by the break time, and the last two weeks even decreasing my resting time did not help, I was behind for 1-2 laps, sometimes even 3.

Even having done half the laps by midday, I could hardly expect the second half of the day to be at the same tempo, as by the end of the day the speed always decreased, plus in the evening I needed the second break. Therefore, to run the same 55 laps in the next 9 hours, I had to shorten the time of my evening rest.

So, during the few weeks that preceded the finish, my evening break lasted no more than 10 minutes. In the evening, hopping inside the van for rest, I said to my helpers that the break was going to be a short one, so we just cooled and stimulated my muscles, which meant that we slightly rubbed my legs with a wet towel to reduce the fatigue, then put some ice in little bags and ran them over my shins or knees to soothe some of the inflammation and cool the legs. Then I got a quick massage for about 3 minutes, and sleep was out of the question. The task was to cover 85 laps by the end of the second break, and to be out of the van no later than 8 pm. Then I had exactly the time needed for the 24 laps to total the required 109 laps for the day.

In the first weeks I was able to catch up with the time if I rested a bit longer and was out at 8:05 pm. However, in the last weeks I preferred to play it safe and was on the course 3-4 minutes before 8 pm. Thus my breaks became shorter and shorter. In the end it looked like this:

- Wake up at 5:00-5:10 am; the car was waiting for me at 5:35.

- Start at 6 am.

- The first break for 25 minutes, the second for 10 minutes. Run until midnight.

- Ride home, shower and give my legs a salt bath. Take honey products (royal jelly, drone brood, ambrosia, pollen and some honey). Jot down the result of the day on my table on the wall, and fall asleep right away. My goal was to be in bed no later than 12:36 am – sometimes it was 12:45 am.

To think how it is possible to move under such a schedule is totally beyond my imagination. Even having gone through it, my mind refuses to understand how the body was able to adapt to such workloads. In this lies the uniqueness of the race: to do what seems to you practically impossible. After the race I knew for sure that there are no limitations in our world, and with the aid of an expansion of consciousness it was possible to go beyond any limitations of the mind. That is what all the participants try to do – to dive into their hearts, to feel the limitlessness of the horizon, to feel oneness with the infinite forces of nature and with the divine forces, then to manifest all that through themselves. Human possibilities are enchanting indeed, and we are destined to know what it truly means to be limitless.

Massage-feast

Occasionally I relaxed my strict discipline – that happened when Hilary or Bahula came and gave me a massage. Then I often added 5 minutes to my daytime break. Saturdays became a real feast: that day both Hilary and Bahula came. Then they gave me a 4-hand massage; I called it a "massage-feast". For such a massage you could run seven days more until the next Saturday.

Speed at the race

My average speed at the race was 7 km per hour. This speed doesn't seem fast even for walking, but when you move during the entire day it happens to be quite a good average speed, and it is not always simple to maintain even that speed. Plus, from this running speed we have to take away the time spent on involuntary technical stops, switching to walking during meals, and the breaks.

One of the situations that very much amused me occurred when a helper forgot to give something to the runner at the food station and, catching up with the runner, she continued to walk alongside. While the runner was running at cruising speed, the helper was walking along in a normal and even

relaxed manner, giving the impression that they were just strolling.

The first time I saw my friend walking peacefully along, while I was running with almost ultimate speed, I could not believe it: was I really running that slowly?. It was almost a shocking experience. Then I asked my friends not to walk but to jog when they were near me – at least it did not remind me of my tortoise speed. On the other hand, observing that scene with the other runners, I laughed heartily, understanding that I was no faster.

Nutrition

During the pre-race dinner cooks gave us a questionnaire about our eating habits and preferences, the necessity for additional portions, and likes and dislikes in foods.

At first I was lost, as I could not recall all the English words for groceries. What I knew for sure was that all the meals would be vegetarian: I had not eaten meat or fish or poultry for 10 years. It turned out that I felt much lighter and better, and also that I could run longer and faster. Based on my own daily diet and experience in multiday running, I was able to remember that I like salads made from fresh vegetables, fruits, berries, freshly-made juices, and I do not eat sweets at the races, as they create inflammation. I remembered that sometimes I could eat pasta with cheese, that I liked buckwheat a lot, but somehow I wrote mostly vegetables and fruits.

The first day passed, then the second, the third... the first week was gone. Going out in the morning I looked at myself for a few moments in the mirror, and soon I noticed that my size had changed a lot. Before the start I gained 3 kg on Suprabha's advice, but all this reserve vanished very soon and it was difficult not to notice that my weight was quickly decreasing. Those coming to the race began to joke, asking if I was eating enough, and then persistently recommended that I eat more.

Dipali is a world and national-record holder in the 6-day race, and an incredibly experienced ultramarathoner. She lives nearby and often visits to support the runners. One day during the daytime break she approached me and literally started to shout, "It's not even a thousand miles, and you've already lost so much weight. Soon you won't have strength and you'll sway from side to side. If you continue like this after the thousand you won't have strength in your muscles." Those words sounded quite convincing but I had no idea how I could stop getting slimmer. It seemed I was eating nonstop as it was, but that was not helping at all. The thing was I had completely stopped eating vegetable oils for half a year. I ate only melted butter – no bread either – so only vegetables, fruits, nuts and grains were left. During the race I continued eating the same way, plus eating a lot of watermelon in the daytime.

Spending more than 10 thousand calories every

day, it is difficult to imagine how to compensate for them. Not only did I not want to eat, but also I could not. Once on Nidhruvi's birthday they made a vegan cake. Pati took a piece for me, but I refused, and she began to persuade me as if I were a little child, to take a little piece, just a bite. Like a capricious girl I agreed only to have one forkful, despite the fact that all my being was literally protesting against it. Summoning up all my will I tried to swallow that piece, but in reply my eyes filled with tears.

Besides, apparently the acid balance had changed in my body, and I could not eat anything with a strong taste, especially sour – I had to take pineapple out of my menu, and even apples, which I like a lot but could not eat at all at the time. Strong tastes, especially sour, made my teeth sensitive to the extreme. It was very painful, so I tried to eat rather mild things, with a neutral taste.

In the afternoon they often brought us a lot of ice cream. It was so tasty that I decided to relax my rule of not eating sweets. The ice cream was in abundance, the real dream of a child – they brought it in huge cups equalling, perhaps, four regular scoops. The first days I swallowed this enormous amount with enjoyment, prolonging the pleasure for three circles. I was glad to have additional calories and did not think of declining this little pleasure. On the fourth day the pleasure went literally sideways. I got a pain in my side – I was hardly running, yet each movement brought pain. That was the last day of the fulfilment of any child's dream – to have ice cream without limits.

Soon we worked out a menu that allowed me to maintain my strength and weight. It had the highest caloric products I could eat. For breakfast I had so-called baby food resembling cooked semolina, always a few sandwiches made from rye bread with seeds and a thick layer of butter with avocado, then fresh berries and fruits, a couple of muesli bars, and some porridge. In between I had some nuts, juice, and yogurt. At about 10 am again I had a few sandwiches with butter and avocado, bananas and a protein cocktail with honey and berries. About the same time I had a spoonful of probiotics or a glass of kefir. After noon I had a proper lunch with soup and salads, then as a second course I often had sweet potatoes or yams, then again a few sandwiches with butter and avocado. We started adding a lot of coconut or olive oil into all the dishes. During the day I ate a lot of watermelon and of course every lap I drank some water or isotonic, or water with salt and sometimes also with honey, and I often ate salty seaweed – it was important to maintain salt balance.

After lunch I often ate yams and sandwiches again. For dinner I had salad with macaroni, once more the protein cocktail, and there were constant snacks with butter, nuts, seaweed and salt. Thus we ran until midnight, and on my way home I always had a big cup of food, then before going to bed I made sure to drink a big mug of warm milk with honey and butter.

Beside that, a few times during the day I had different honey products, including honey itself, ambrosia, pollen, royal jelly, drone brood, plus magnolia-vine berries. Those were my little secrets that helped to maintain strength and energy. I strongly felt the effect of the magnolia-vine berries and I simply liked to take honey products. I really

believed and felt that they were good for me, that they would help. I had begun to take them during my training. The very fact that in training I had been able to endure great loads and feel good gave me belief in those magic honey products.

After the first two weeks my helpers went to the ayurvedic doctor, Dr Kumar, and he gave me some herb powder that helped me not to lose weight anymore. Everything worked: that powder, my high-calorie diet and protein products helped me to stabilize my weight.

Every week, one of the race directors, Sandhani, came in the afternoon to weigh all the runners. Usually he came in the evening, when it was dark, to ride a bicycle around the course, but when he came in the afternoon I guessed the weighing was at hand. He took out his writing pad and jotted down the weight of each runner. Then he told us the result of the last week – of which I was mightily afraid – and it was clear, how much weight you lost. Thus the organizers made sure nobody crossed the mark of losing more than 10% of their weight. I think almost all of the runners were close to that number, but as I approached it I tried by all means to compensate for the calories burned.

However, the loss of weight was not a problem for all the runners – there were those easily able to maintain their weight or even slightly gain more. I noticed that such runners kept a stable speed that did not go down towards the end of the race. However, not all participants established the connection of weight with speed. One runner, for example, never made himself eat if he did not want to. The less your weight, the quicker you run, and there is no reason to make yourself eat if you do not want to. That theory works fine for him, and by the end of the race he becomes slim as a fallow deer and runs with the speed of a deer. The main thing is to find what works for you.

Pranjal has his own rituals in eating: each morning before the start he takes a big pack of juice and a big Snickers bar; sometimes he drinks coffee, saying that he hates the taste and smell of coffee but it helps him to wake up. Near lunchtime he drinks a bottle of alcohol-free beer, and when evening sets in he takes from the fridge a can of energy drink. Stutisheel eats soy products during the race, and in the evening he likes to recharge with a plate of Chinese noodles. Before going to bed he often drinks a protein cocktail and likes kombucha – a drink resembling tea fungus that many grow at home. I also have kombucha on the list of my favourites – I even chose it as a treat for all the runners after my finish.

We also did some experiments with adding essential oils to water. I was advised to try adding a drop of mint oil to two litres of water, to perk myself up when very sleepy. It turned out that even a drop was strongly felt in such a big volume, and when I accidentally added 2-3 drops, it was almost impossible to drink, but it worked immediately and the sleep went away at once.

Plus, a few times Stutisheel shared with me his special eyedrops that caused an instant invigorative and sobering effect. When I tried them for the first time, I called to all the gods in the whole world and literally shouted why I had this punishment. Not only could I not imagine such a strong stinging, but

also I did not think it was possible to endure it. In return the drops did their work 100% – I did not want to sleep until the very evening; the emotions were overflowing.

Hydration

Hydration at this race is as important as anything else. In hot weather the body of the runner loses much of its salts and minerals, therefore it is necessary to replenish the losses with liquids containing salts and minerals. Coconut water was one of the favourite drinks – it is a natural isotonic – a wonderful drink for physical strains, with a very pleasant neutral taste and an excellent source of minerals in a wide variety.

Beside that, during the day – starting from 10 am and finishing at 9 pm – I took 5 tablets called *Heat Guard*, which helped to deal with the heat. Those tablets, covered with a light-coloured shell, contained a huge amount of salt – probably a teaspoonful. Once I bit through the tablet and nearly spat it out – so much salt was in my mouth, it was almost impossible to hold. With difficulty I swallowed it, drinking lots of water, but those tablets wonderfully helped me to deal with the heat and to stay conscious, not melting away under 30 degrees centigrade: they replenished all the salts that came out of the body.

One more source of minerals was *Trace Mineral* drops – an extract of minerals from seawater, an unbelievably helpful and wholly natural product. We dissolved the drops in water and added lemon or orange juice, but the taste of the drops was so awful that it was impossible to overpower it by any other taste. I winced like anything, but drank it without any further persuasion.

One day there was heavy rain that would not stop for the entire day. The weather was cool, and the rain went on a long time; from time to time a strong wind was blowing. I ran in a light windbreaker, and took my umbrella when the rain was getting heavier. There was so much water around, and the air temperature was not high. I did not want to drink at all and occasionally I started to skip drinking, never taking more than one cup per lap, so I did not notice in the least how the dehydration came. I felt it clearly by the end of the day, when my whole body began to burn. It had happened quite a few times before, and almost always the temperature of my body rose by the evening. Putting my palm on the other hand I felt the heat in the body, but that evening the temperature was obviously rising higher than usual. I felt the heat not only on the skin, but also inside my body, and with that a feeling of fatigue came. Almost all the next day the feelings were the same, despite the fact that we realized our mistake and I began to drink ample quantities.

Dehydration is difficult to notice in time; therefore it is better to find your own need for liquid at a given amount of workload and never to forget

about replenishing liquids, including water and isotonic drinks. The drinks could be ready-made or made by the runner. In my case the basic drinks, except water, were coconut water and water with salt, honey and lemon juice. To vary the flavour, it is possible to add different juices to the drink.

Trying to avoid dehydration I consumed a large enough quantity of liquids and, sure enough, the reverse side of it was the necessity to frequently visit a 'green cabin' – the toilet. That also required time, as one cannot visit it in less than a minute. A distinctive feature of my body was that I had to make the visits oftener than others, and that frequency went progressively higher in relation to the quantities of liquid drunk. Sometimes I had to go to the toilet every two laps – that is, every 20 minutes – which amounted to a great deal of time during the day. I tried to drink less, but then my body immediately overheated; my breath became very hot, I felt the heat coming from inside – as a result the speed went down and that was a stress for the entire body. After long experiments with volumes of drinking I came to the conclusion that it was better to drink as much as I needed, even though it meant losses of time for the toilet. In return it served as a source of jokes with Nidhruvi. Even if sometimes I was overtaking her at the course, after the camp and the toilet, I saw her back again in front of me. Then, on approaching her, we both began laughing.

Equipment

Ten T-shirts, seven pairs of shorts, fifteen pairs of socks, sun block, a hat, sunglasses, a plastic raincoat and an umbrella – what else do you need for a race in hot weather? It turned out, a lot of things. During the race, with my mobile phone in hand, I ordered from online shops everything that suddenly became necessary – among the first things I bought were a few pairs of compression calf and arm sleeves. I used the calf sleeves to avoid injuries, putting them on in the morning when my muscles were still cold and stiff after the night's rest. In the mornings the body needed some time to adjust to the rhythm of my running, and my body needed that time to become more flexible. I felt more protected while wearing the calf sleeves; it seemed that they helped to prevent injuries. In the evening it was vice versa: the body was already tired, but it was in the evening when a new inspiration was born and I got my 'second wind' – or my tenth for that matter – and the speed went up considerably. Plus, the time created pressure, and I wanted to run the required laps: i.e. in the evenings the speed went up. Then the calf sleeves helped to keep my muscles in tone and to avoid injuries in tired legs, when the soul rushes quicker than the body.

The compression sleeves are made of a rather thin breathable material. For the arms I chose white ones. During the heat soaking them with water helped considerably to cool my body and to protect my skin from sunburn.

One of the first orders was also the purchase

of sea salt. In the evening I tried to take a regular bath with a big quantity of the salt, or a little warm bath for my feet. I liked to take a regular warm bath the most, as it was quicker: I was able to wash simultaneously. Sometimes we added baking soda or hydrogen peroxide. By the end of the race the water in our house was lukewarm for some reason, and I did not feel like taking a proper bath. Then we got a bucket and I put my feet in it, sitting on my bed. I was totally relaxed at such moments – my feet were glad and my body felt much better. Those moments were bliss itself. After the foot bath Pati massaged me and I fell asleep during the massage, in 3-5 minutes. When it was necessary for me to turn onto my stomach, for the massage of the backs of my legs or for oiling, I was awakened, and having turned, fell asleep again instantly. Body oiling also became one of the more pleasant rituals. My body got essential minerals and moisture through the skin. Coconut oil, which we used most of the time, was absorbed in seconds. The skin ceased to be oily in less than a minute.

Sunblock turned out to be one of the most necessary things – for me it was like air or water, and I applied it daily to the skin on my face, arms, legs, ears and neck. Some runners did not use the cream at all. Vasu and Yuri used it only when duly asked, on the days when the sun blazed as in the desert. After I heard Bahula's words about burnt skin, that it was an additional stress and that the body had to fight it and spend its strength, there was no more need to persuade me to use sunblock. On the contrary, if we forgot to apply sunblock after the break, I would ask my helpers to bring it to the midpoint of the course

– the spot where we did everything we forgot to do at the camp. The helpers could reach the spot easily. It was just 60-70 meters across from the camp and they were there in time while I was running some 400 meters at my tortoise pace.

It turned out that one hat is not enough. It is better to have two as a minimum – it is easier to wash them that way. The hats I chose transformed easily from regular ones to ones with wide brims, generously protecting the neck, ears and even shoulders from the sun.

On hot days I often used a cotton kerchief, tying it around my neck. Before putting it on I soaked it in cold water, and its coolness went into my body, giving a lot of pleasant sensations. It helped to cool the body nicely, and for that I needed to pour water on the kerchief quite often, as it dried quickly.

As I have written previously, I had to choose new socks. The socks that finally suited me were synthetic ones with thick heels and toes, which gave a pleasant feeling of softness, while the other parts were made from a thin material. I used the biggest size – L for men, in order to reduce pressure on my feet – but next time I would probably choose M. As for the number of pairs – the more the better, but obviously not less than 6-7 pairs.

To the list of possible equipment, I would add a special sun-protection suit. Ananda-Lahari used one: it was very light and protected the skin from sunburn very well. It can be a real salvation in hot weather. It consists of a light jacket and trousers fully covering the body. The material does not allow UV through, preventing against skin burns.

***Cooling kerchief around my neck, and hat,
protecting from the sun on my head***

Raincoats were also popular with the runners – they are very light and thin and will protect against strong or persistent rain, not allowing the clothes underneath to get soaked. Some runners had their pants cut below the knees, as it helped the skin to breathe.

Raincoats were of different colors. Once Nidhruvi and I and ran together, and her raincoat was yellow, while mine was blue. Underneath we had T-shirts of different colors. Approaching the camp we started to laugh loudly, as Nidhruvi joked, "In such multicolored clothes I feel like a clown, and now it is time for our performance." We burst out laughing: true, all we lacked were clownish noses.

68

That year we had frequent rain, but gradually we got used to it. Most important was to have a plan of action for rain. I chose a simple algorithm: during heavy rain I put on my raincoat and took an umbrella – a wide one, or medium-sized. Sometimes I left out some part of the rain costume; it depended on the intensity of the rain, its duration and the temperature of the air. It was very good if my feet were oiled during the rain with coconut oil, but I never stopped for that specifically. Sure, while it was raining there was no sense in changing shoes or clothes. As soon as the rain stops and the biggest puddles are drained, it is time to dry your feet and powder them with baby or talcum powder, and put on dry running shoes. Talc helps the wetness to be absorbed, thus preventing the skin from getting sore with friction and possible blistering.

During the rain everybody chooses their own garments

Fire in my running shoes

From the very beginning I met with a problem that was unknown and new for me. As early as the third day, my feet began to burn unbearably – a painful sensation came every time I put my feet on the concrete and the feet got excruciatingly hot. They were swollen – I had the feeling that they had been inflated with an air pump, and the skin became very sensitive. On one hand each step was unbelievably painful and touchy, and on the other hand I wanted to massage my feet despite the pain it caused. In those moments it seemed to me that the sensation was most unbearable, as my feet took the weight of my entire body. We tried different ways of solving the problem, and they all helped in some way, so I could continue to move.

Vasu from St. Petersburg advised me to cut some soft grass and put it under my feet, inside my socks. At first that idea seemed quite amusing, but soon I was ready to try any means in the hope that something would work. The grass helped, it brought certain relief and took away the heat. It looked a bit funny when I took off my socks before the massage and there was the grass inside, as if it had grown there. It worked to a certain extent, although it did not solve the problem completely. The burning sensation still persisted.

Pranjal gave me his neem oil – it has a cooling and soothing effect – and we started to apply it before going to sleep.

We put some baby powder or talc into my socks in order to reduce friction, plus we used special cooling sprays for sports, but all of that was not enough. Dipali advised me to make a supplementary insert for the insoles of my running shoes, to shift the pressure from the forefoot to the midfoot.

The fact that I already had a special heel cushion insert to protect my Achilles tendons provoked an even greater shift of load to the frontal part of my feet, and brought an acute sensation of burning – sometimes it seemed like I had a fire in my running shoes. We stuck the insert under the arch, behind the ball of the foot, following the toes. Thus, when I landed, some of the pressure was distributed to the new artificial cushion. It helped considerably, although when the cushion accidentally moved forward the pain became unbearable, as the pressure to the painful areas increased.

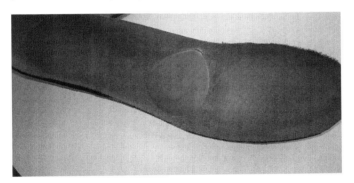

Insole with insert that can be purchased or cut from old insoles

During the breaks I always put my feet in a basin of cold water with ice. It brought unbelievable relief, although afterwards we had to redo all the foot tapes, as they came unstuck. Once we were advised of a simple solution – to put my feet into a

plastic bag first, and only then into the basin. It is so easy, but even such logical ideas don't come to you all at once.

We continued to look for means of dealing with the fire in my running shoes. Somebody said that toxins come out of the feet, in order to cleanse the body. Others believed that I should 'outlive' the burning – that soon my body would get used to local weather, to pressure, and everything would be easier. It was very difficult and painful to wait, but I had no choice.

Bahula was providing medical aid for the girls during the multi-day races – she has an incredible longstanding experience in the field. Once she suggested changing socks. Previously I had tried dozens of socks for sports, and had chosen simple Russian cotton ones – they suited me the best and I always took pride in the fact that I could do with dollar socks. I brought 17 pairs of them. It turned out that the cotton held the moisture – although seemingly dry to the touch, in reality they were damp. Such material rubbed my skin sore, resulting in my feet burning in the hot weather. So I had to change the socks. I asked to choose a long pair with the thinnest material. In the evening I was given the only option from the nearest sports shop – a short model with some terry lining on the heels and feet. But I was ready to try anything in the hope that something would work. Surprisingly, those new socks really helped, and I was all right with the terry lining. Such a small thing could change so much. It considerably relieved the pain in my feet, and soon the pain was gone completely. You never know what is going to work, and it is absolutely necessary to try different things. Some key is bound to open the lock in question. What is important is to try all the keys and not to turn down any option.

Each step is a new horizon

On the eleventh day of the race, when I saw on the result board the number of miles I had run – about 680 – I suddenly realized that I had never run that far. Before that time my maximum had been 675 miles, three years earlier at the 10-day race. Now with each new step I did what I had never done before, something completely new, and with every step I became a new person, someone quite different from who I was even a second ago.

It was an unfamiliar feeling: I continued to run around the same circle and outwardly the same things were happening that had taken place the day before, but I was becoming someone new from that moment on.

For me outer achievements are manifestations of inner personal qualities, of an inner state of conscious. To be able to run farther, longer or faster, you have to be ready both physically and psychologically. You have to endure on all levels. That meant that with every step I became stronger, got to know something new that I had not known

before, felt what I had never felt before.

All these feelings made my head spin, and my determination to run further only increased.

The race of surrender

I like to call this race the Race of Surrender – surrender of one's will to something higher, to the Divine Will. In daily life at every moment I have a choice in front of me, and I constantly make decisions on what to think about, what to do, who to communicate with, how to act. Certainly I do not always know if I am making the right choice – the exception is in the cases when one receives a special signal or a clear inner message, coming so spontaneously and distinctly that it becomes totally impossible to miss it. However, sometimes the decisions come at the level of habits – mechanically or intuitively.

The race... here everything is so simple, I know exactly what to do, what I am here for – I only have to move forward and be happy.

Here, I absolutely forget about my own desires; they all merge with the soul's aspiration. It is one of the few cases when I am utterly certain that what I am doing is right; it gives joy to my inner being. There comes a clear feeling inside, that this race has a special meaning not only for the runners themselves, but also for the entire world: it definitely inspires a large number of people and proves that a heart full of faith can manifest its boundlessness. Then only the sky can be the limit for a human being.

End of Ramadan at the race

During the race the runners became the witnesses to many events in the lives of the local people, and one of the days coincided with the end of the Muslim holy day Ramadan. In the neighborhood live representatives of different religions and nationalities: Latin Americans, Hindus, Muslims. Thousands of Muslims were gathering at the stadium inside the course that morning, all of them wearing festive national dress. On the field by the stadium they arranged themselves in neat rows: men in the front and women behind them at some distance. There gathered about ten thousand participants, who knelt down side by side. At some moment they grew quiet, and it was so still that the air seemed to vibrate with deep silence. A few moments later there came prayerful singing from the stage. Then all of them offered their simultaneous prayer to Allah, bowing their heads to the earth. That moment the air around was permeated with a deep, sincere prayerful worship of the divine. It was an incredibly

sincere feeling coming from the very heart. I thought then that all the gods of the earth, representing the Hindu, the Muslim, and the Christian creeds, gathered there at that comparatively small ground in a seemingly unremarkable area of Queens, in the city of New York. I continued to run and for a long time inside me there was an inner call to the divine presence to stay inside me, that I could always feel it and be guided by it, and be led in the right direction at every moment of my life.

Oneness with the world around

The landscape of the course may seem quite simple to many onlookers. The distance goes around a college; there is a busy road at one side and there are sports grounds inside the loop – with school children, adults and little kids playing. The favorite game of the school children and adults is handball. The ball hits the concrete wall and bounces back to the player. It closely resembles squash, only the ball is made of rubber and is hit with the player's hand (girls sometimes use rackets like those used for tennis but smaller). It looks very simple, but watching the beginners you realize that here, too, players need skill and practice. The game is very popular in America – what can be simpler than to buy a dollar ball and find a concrete wall. Of course, it is better to stock up on a few balls: many a time I witnessed how this rubber friend went under the wheels of a passing car, exploding with a bang and the players could not help but get yet another ball. During the race they held two large handball competitions – one for men and one for women – with players from all over New York City. On those days the fans positioned themselves around the perimeter of the field, along the fence and, sure enough, on the sidewalks where we ran. There were grilled sausages there, alcoholic beverages on sale, the loud music blared and everybody was having a good time. The first day I was not very happy with what was going on. I involuntarily thought that now I had to avoid bumping into the spectators walking around, and that I did not like such music, and I was not the greatest fan of the smoke from the grills. But as soon as I had such thoughts I felt there was something wrong with them. After all, these spectators could also have wondered why these runners bustle in and out between their rows, blocking the view. But it seemed that they did not mind it at all.

Then the next moment I tried to feel that we all are one: let the handball players choose a different game, but we all are on one common field – the earth – and there is something that unites all of us. After that, a feeling of harmony and oneness came to me, the feeling of unity with the whole world – with the smell of sausages or the fragrance of lilac, with overcrowded sidewalks for me to run on, or empty gardens with the fragrance of roses. The world is as it is, and I would like to take it as it is, without criticizing it. If the world were absolutely

perfect, it would probably not need my love.

Handball tournament day – the runners become a part of the event and merge with the flow of people

After such thoughts it became much easier to run through the crowd of the fans: now inwardly they were my friends. Once, having tripped over somebody's foot and falling down, I was able to maintain a balanced inner state and not to get upset. Thus the weekends went by, with handball and baseball tournaments, student graduation and the end of Ramadan. On those days the sidewalks were full of people, the road overcrowded with cars, and we became a part of the events. But now I did not divide the world into the runners and everybody else. We were a part of one big Universe, the players of one big game – the oneness game – and it became much easier to live without tension, to live with joy.

Balls on the course

Some runners very much liked to play with a ball while running: hitting it on the concrete and catching it again. Such balls are used for the game of handball. They can be of different colors, and running with them adds a change to the routine. Running becomes a game – it seems that you are not running but simply playing with the ball. It can be one of the ways to distract oneself from the pain and discomfort, and to become a child enjoying a game.

One runner often ran with a ball during the day. He was quite skilled with it: he could throw the ball with such precision that after a few steps he caught it again. Once his helper bought many balls of different colors, and I chose two of them – a yellow one and a blue one. I decided to run in such a manner too. It was fun, but proved to be much more difficult than it seemed from the outside. In my case the ball often flew in quite an unexpected direction, and to run after it was too difficult a task, as I had to run sideways and the moves were obviously not in an optimal trajectory. So I decided to try something else.

Among multiple surprises, brought to me twice in suitcases from Moscow, I found a ball. The ball was made of soft rubber. It slightly changed its form when squeezed, and its purpose was to develop the fine motor skills of children, when they compress it in their hands. It was a gift from my friend in Moscow. I really liked running with the ball and squeezing it in my hands, which helped me to stay away from the

thoughts I did not want to enter into my mind. With that ball it was very easy for the mind to remain in complete silence. How simple can be the solution to many problems. I really like simplicity in life – it seems that it works in many cases, concerning the approach to life, attitude and relationships between people.

The power of a smile

When I recall what state and mood accompanied me during my running, the words *joy* and *lightness* appear right away. Before the beginning of the race I had read one of the talks given by Sri Chinmoy on the race. I especially liked one paragraph, and it went into my very heart. Sri Chinmoy recalled that when he had come to the race and offered the runners some ice cream or other prasad (the food blessed by a spiritual Master), one of the runners, despite his deadly fatigue, had always smiled and said, "Thank you".

Sri Chinmoy said, that if we could smile even in the most difficult moments, then that smile would immensely help us to cover the distance, and in the inner world it would be a real divine victory. These words went deep into my heart and accompanied me during the entire race.

Preparing myself for that journey, I first dreamt of a victory in the inner world – I wanted my inner state, mood and consciousness to please my soul. In other words, I aspired for that victory in the inner world, the victory over myself. Having read Sri Chinmoy's writings on smiling, I thought that if there was such an easy way to please the highest in me – to smile – then I would definitely do that. Those words always stayed inside me and even in the most difficult moments I tried to smile. Then it was much easier not to plunge into the body's pain, not to concentrate my attention on it, but instead to stay in my heart.

At one moment during the race a secret opened itself to me – perhaps, I had known it before, but here it was presented unusually vividly. I understood that the positive approach to life – a feeling of joy and a harmonious soulful mood – had a positive impact on the physical state. It even cured traumas. When I fly on the wings of joy, when I do not think of my problems, and do not bury myself in my own thoughts, then no traumas can appear, and this effect is even prolonged. I am sure that to a great extent I finished due to a smile that was always inside. That became a most effective painkiller and an anti-inflammatory medicine.

I surely wanted to finish in the given time limit, but I passed the responsibility – in terms of the result in miles and place – to the higher forces. In the first half of the race I realized at one point that there was a tension inside me: I felt that an apprehension virus lived somewhere inside of me. I was afraid that I might get a serious injury, causing me to walk for a few days, and then I would not be able

to finish in time. Those thoughts were unconscious and not even formed as thoughts as such, but they existed somewhere and I disliked that feeling. I wanted the tension to go away from all levels of my consciousness. Such thoughts could never bring anything positive; they only limit the outer and inner speed, and slow down progress. Having felt how my entire being strained at the thought of an injury, I tried to let my worries go. I understood that whatever happened was only an experience that I had to go through – an experience that would make me stronger – and if I felt pain, then the higher part of my being felt that pain thousands of times stronger. Then I felt very profoundly and strongly that I was never alone – someone infinitely more powerful than me was always near. Whatever tests I was to meet, I would be given the strength to endure. So I would try to do my best and to be receptive to the Light and Energy that were flowing through me. The result was not my responsibility – only a sincere and conscious effort was required of me.

Could I presume to know what the real purpose of my participation was in the race, and what I was meant to learn in those 52 days? The moment I consciously let all responsibility for the miles go away, all tension and thoughts of whether I would be able to finish in time disappeared. That moment I felt light-hearted and was able to let all my worries go. At once joy came, and anxiety disappeared like a balloon set free by a child, speedily going up to the sky and vanishing in the clouds.

Chapter without a title

When asked if it is boring to run in so little a circle for so long, I cannot remember being bored even once. Each of those 10,000 circles was different, while outwardly remaining almost without change. They were different due to the fact that I myself was constantly changing and my goals were different in different periods of the race. First I had to adjust to the rhythm of the race, then to be able to cope with outer difficulties – to adapt to unusual weather conditions, and then to be able to maintain the speed. Outer events such as Ramadan festivities, baseball tournaments, my friends' arrivals, changes in weather, introduced a constant diversity, and those events became significant outwardly, but inner changes turned out to be even more interesting.

My attitude towards the miles covered was changing, as well as my expectation of taking a certain place. Gradually there came the capacity to stay in the present moment – to think only of one step, one lap, and not to worry how many days and miles were in front of me, even if that day I had run fewer miles than were required. There also came the capacity not to be offended by the people around me, to calmly accept unfulfilled expectations, and even not to expect per se. Not to expect actions, words, letters, reactions and to be glad about the simplest things – a joyful sticker on a food cup, the smile of a passer-by, a singing bird or a rainbow in the sky. Those days of running return me to simple human values; they sweep away all the dust collecting on

the aureole of my heart in the daily routine, full of hustle and bustle. Those days remind me again that happiness and joy are everywhere around us, if only we want to see them. What is important is to thrust open the shutters of our windows to the morning sun, and not to hide in our little room limited by the walls built by ourselves. The sun is always ready to share its light with everyone.

Long before my participation in the race, while coming to New York, I had always been eager to get to that course and have a walk or a jog on that concrete, now sacred. Those eight hundred meters, harder than the hardest for the feet and most dear to the heart, are really sacred: one cannot imagine the level of energy around that college. So many prayers, emotions, deep inner and outer experiences were offered, felt and gone through. How sincerely and deeply the runners were praying to all kinds of higher forces – hour by hour, day by day, and year by year. How much sweat, blood and tears each of the runners left on this course. For me everyone who comes to the start of the race is indeed a hero. Knowing all the difficulties lying in front of them, they venture that step for high inner goals and aspirations that are far outside the realm of getting a prize, monetary reward or fame. At the finish line the participants get a medal, a plastic trophy and a T-shirt. After returning home, perhaps a couple of local newspapers would write about this stereotype-shattering race and of how many pairs of running shoes each participant had worn out in 52 days. Those one and a half months changes the life of each runner. But deep inside, each one believes that those days change not only their lives

– there is a hope inside that it is also important for someone else who dreams about going beyond customary stereotypes, even if he lives thousands of miles away in another corner of the globe, and they do not know each other. What if another crazy enthusiast would think that he also has the same two arms, two legs and a head, and if those fourteen people can do such things, then he would be able to achieve his goal too. What if he would believe that he is stronger than his fears and would want to try something he thinks is unreachable? And then, upon learning about this race, he may be filled with new determination. What if the runners' prayers about peace, friendship and the oneness of people from different countries and continents would be heard by the Creator, by the One who can fulfill these prayers? Or, what if this little paradise present at the course, when all the participants wish each other only good, share smiles, the heart's oneness, love and support, would start to distribute itself to the world around and help this planet to become a bit better, kinder and more perfect – even a little? For this, doubtlessly, each one coming to the start is ready to run. Such feelings and hopes help and maintain the motivation to move forward.

Letters of support

There came a lot of letters of support; Sahishnu, one of the race directors, brought and distributed them twice a day. When he appeared with a pile of papers I always hoped there would be a few that he would hand out to me or to my helper. I liked it best when he handed them to me personally – it resembled the way a regular mailman brings a letter and you are eager to open and read it.

Mom is reading some letters while running

A great deal of letters I got from my friends, work colleagues and, to my big surprise, from perfect strangers. A few people whom I got to know during the race through their e-mails kept writing to me all the time and I was even looking forward to their letters. After a few messages, it turned out that with one particular girl, Ann, we had done a few of the same competitions, but we had never spoken to each other. She sent me a few proper stories, not just a page long – how I wished I could reply with adequate length-letters, although it was not an easy task to text and write mail on the go.

Daily letters of support brought so many emotions. Oftentimes they were full of good jokes that I shared with the other runners and we had a hearty laugh together, or it was an inspiring quote helping to maintain motivation, or some interesting story that made the laps go by in the twinkling of an eye. The letters served as real messengers, bringing not only a few lines on paper, but also a huge portion of kindness, love and support from people at different locations around the globe.

Letters always inspire

Nidhruvi

The Austrian participant Nidhruvi and I became very good friends. It turned out that we had already run together in a multiday race, but we had not been able to meet then. When we had met on the eve of the 3100, Nidhruvi came up to me laughing – and her laugh was always so contagious that I myself had a good laugh in reply. So began our acquaintance, and in that manner it proceeded. In the morning oftentimes we ran a few laps together – or even a few hours. Time and again we laughed seeing each other in the car on our way to the starting line, as without any agreement we had put on T-shirt and shorts of the same colors. Once we had pale blue shorts and bright pink T-shirt on – not everyone would call such colors matching. We joked that our souls communicate at night and agree on what to wear next morning. It often happened that the counters mixed us up with each other – we were two blondes of a similar build, with rather short hair arranged in ponytails. We really felt oneness with each other, and Nidhruvi even told me once that she felt an inner connection with Russia. We taught each other funny words both in Russian and German, and then surprised our helpers by producing merry phrases in the language unknown to them. Beside the standard set of greetings and partings Nidhruvi learned how to say, "Let's dance." in Russian. She would run past my helpers and make such an unexpected offer, and start to waltz. It all was marvellously amusing, greatly helping to take our minds off the problems and pains, using the best natural remedy in the world – laughter.

Morning laps with Nidhruvi

It is always easy and joyful to run with a person close to you in spirit, and the laps fly by noticeably faster.

Most of all, I admired Nidhruvi's unbending spirit. She had already finished the race in 2013. This time not everything went easily. There were injuries, and on some days she could not run the required miles. Despite that, her faith always stayed with her. Each morning Nidhruvi was determined to catch up on the necessary miles. Not even once did she yield to despair or apathy; on the contrary, she always kept her faith and optimism.

It is much easier to maintain these qualities when everything goes well. I think it was easier for me to remain cheerful, as my average daily pace was almost always enough for me to finish in time. Sometimes I asked myself whether I could go to the course smiling every day, if I understood that it

would be hard for me to finish. Nidhruvi's example always inspired me very much. She showed the spirit of a real hero who marches forward and would never give up, and in the end would gratefully receive any result. She gave her all until the very last moment of those 52 days, and her race indeed proved to be a real victory – the victory of the spirit.

The value of time

For this race not only is speed important, but also the pace. That includes how quickly the runners can pass the food station, how often they stop at a given lap, how often and for how long they switch to walking, and even how quick they are in the WC – every second is important at the race. Often the race directors even call it the race of discipline.

During the first few days it was not easy for me to maintain a good pace. I wanted to stop and stretch more often, and even psychologically I had to get used to staying at the course all day long.

Once I noticed that Pranjal's speed was not much faster than mine, but by the end of the day he always had about 15 more laps. How was that possible? Sure, there were many other runners who ran many more laps than me, but their speed was strikingly different – they ran much faster. In the case of Pranjal, although his speed was faster, it was not that much faster.

It was obvious that he had a very structured schedule of running, not wasting a second. From time to time I tried to keep running behind him for a few laps. I ran some 30-50 meters behind to keep an eye on him. Then I saw what not wasting time really meant. At the food station he took two cups of water or a cup of food and a cup of water, then emptied them while walking 10 to 15 meters and immediately continued to run. It all happened so quickly that it was hard to imagine whether it would be possible to do the same any quicker. His movements were always precise, swift and concentrated, even if he was tired and it was the end of the day. After a few days of observation and attempts to repeat something like that, it seemed that I managed to learn how to treat time attentively and not to waste seconds.

It so happened that when I ran with another runner, sometimes I was able to pass the food station quicker, then I stopped to stretch and waited for them. During such times I asked myself if I was acting correctly. On the one hand I could have run faster; on the other hand we were all friends and, of course, it is good to support a close friend. But once an answer came by itself – it was as follows:

One day from the very morning I had a painful shin. I could run, but I was so close to getting an injury that I could not think of anything else. All my attention was focused on how to keep moving, how to make one more step, one more lap. That day I talked to all kinds of forces of nature, asking the

huge trees that grew along the course for energy and the sky for lightness. For a reason I will explain later, I was holding in my hand a piece of bark, and that was helping me. All my concentration was focused on running and on my inner state. In my visualizations I imagined how feeling light helped me to cope with the injuries, how it dissolved all pain. I regularly stretched to aid the blood circulation and thus remove inflammation. Of course it took extra time, and I was saving every possible second while passing the food station – that day I almost did not speak. On my headphones I listened to beautiful music; inside me there was only its tune and my heartbeat. My heart was calling for only one thing – to move forward as fast as possible. I remember that day so vividly. All of it was one flow, and miraculously in the afternoon I was able to move at a steady and even pace. By the end of that day I had completed exactly my 109 required laps. I was so happy, and felt incredible satisfaction and fulfillment. That evening I thanked the Universe for every step and lap, and asked that the next day would be free of pain.

My prayers were heard and the next morning was pleasantly without pain. I was extremely glad that my shin was better. That gave me some relaxation and I was running without much tension. At mid-morning, Nidhruvi and I ran some laps together and then again in the afternoon. We laughed a lot, joked and shared funny stories, then laughed some more and did not notice how we had slowed down. Instead of increasing the pace together, we spent more time waiting for each other, stretching and joking with the helpers. Once Vasu passed us and we continued to laugh, so he asked us why we were laughing so much and running so slowly. Our reply also was by way of a joke, and between us we mentioned that men could not laugh and were always too serious.

At the end of the day a surprise was waiting for me: I was two laps short, despite the fact that no physical pain had bothered me that day. How was it possible? The previous day I was on the verge of an injury and still was able to run the 109 required laps, and today was painless but I ran fewer laps? That day made me think of the value of time. If I was given the speed and ability to run quickly, then it was not to be neglected. One must value the time, speed and capacity offered by the present moment. If somebody is running ahead or behind, no fear – each one moves at his own pace – but it would not be wise to waste the capacity to move to the goal quickly.

Energy is in movement

When you spend 18 hours a day on the course, plus spend some time getting ready in the morning, time in the car and, of course, the evening shower or foot bath or even the regular bath, you have only 4 hours left for sleep. If all went well I was lucky to have 4 hours and 15 minutes. That time was enough and I never felt I was falling down for lack of sleep. I started drinking coffee only during the last two

weeks to hearten myself a bit. Nevertheless, the whole time I had a dream to sleep for at least half an hour more one day. On the other hand, I could not leave the course without having completed 109 laps before midnight – those 109 laps were always a priority in comparison to sleep. I hoped that if I finished 109 laps by 11:30 I would definitely go home half an hour early, and would not even run until midnight. The runners decided for themselves when to go home. The only requirement was to get to the starting line at 6 am. Sometimes I managed to complete 109 laps 10-15 minutes earlier, but those 15 minutes would not be a noticeable addition to my sleep, so I stayed until midnight.

It seemed that the dream of a good sleep or at least a longer one, would remain unfulfilled, but once, luck smiled on me and I was in bed at 12:15 – an unbelievable achievement. It was especially valuable for me, as back home in Moscow I had always tried to go to sleep no later than 11 pm. After that, every 30 minutes made a big difference. I could never imagine myself living on 6 hours of sleep for two months. Usually two weeks of sleep of less than 7 hours affected me. It seemed like a real miracle that I could endure all those miles on a 4-hour sleep regimen.

So it is absolutely true that energy comes from movement. What is important is to keep moving forward all the time and then the energy for that movement will definitely come.

To share an umbrella

I remember two stories connected with rain and my umbrella during the race. Once, I think it was on US Independence Day, we had some visitors from neighboring towns. Two young women who visit the race every year stood near a big beautiful flowerbed just next to the base camp. First they approvingly and eagerly clapped their hands, and then they started singing with great enthusiasm. It was so nice and joyful. We could feel a new flow of energy on the course. I was always glad when people came and smiled and waved their hands or clapped – basically offering their good will. A passer-by could simply wave, but for me it was a big deal. Such a simple thing would give one strength for many a lap. So, the rain began suddenly and it seemed that those women did not mind at all. They continued to sing and clap. Then the rain became a downpour and I decided to put on the windbreaker from my rain suit. During the short stop needed for that, I asked my helper Pati to give the girls my big umbrella to protect them from the downpour. I so much wanted to offer something to those souls in return for their encouragement and support on the course, that the entire next lap I could not think of anything else but to hope Pati had given them the umbrella before they left the course. Seeing them at the end of the lap, singing under the big green and white canopy of the umbrella, I was ready to jump for joy – pity I could not jump anymore – but I was so glad to be of help to other people that this little incident gave me strength for the entire evening.

That is why they say that to give presents is more enjoyable than to receive them.

The second umbrella episode was the other way around. Early on the morning of a rainy day I noticed a woman with a funny umbrella that looked like a big green leaf of a tropical plant, with a handle made from bamboo. The woman sang for us every morning in the group 'Enthusiasm Awakeners'. I at once imagined a grasshopper that had improvised a shelter from the rain. I called to the woman, greeted her and said that she had a very nice umbrella. Later I saw her a few times during their performance and when I looked at her umbrella, I involuntarily began smiling. But I did not expect to see, after some laps, my mom holding that very umbrella. My mom merrily told me that the umbrella was a gift for me from that lady. Such a surprise. Indeed, the earth is round, and whatever we do or think is bound to return to us with double force.

The race of self-giving

When I think about the race, there are so many inner ways to define it, but first of all it is a race of self-giving. It all starts with the race organizers. Most likely, the runners do not even realize all the organizational subtleties. I will write only about things I saw myself, but I am sure that is not even half of the organizers' concerns.

The chief race director, Rupantar, began his day at 4 am, coming to the camp site and unloading the vans with the 14 runners' personal belongings: boxes of shoes, which each runner had under their table, a few smaller boxes with personal belongings such as creams and sprays, etc., plus a chair. On the long table (the favorite of the runners), Rupantar put out breakfast that he had brought from the race kitchen. The girls started preparing food in the kitchen at 5 am. After the camp was set, Rupantar went to pick up the runners coming by car. Amongst the lucky ones were all the girls and Stutisheel, a veteran of the race. Arriving at the course, the runners had to get ready for the start within a few minutes. Some shaved, some cut their running shoes, and some checked the printout with the results of the previous day, which were put on the runners' tables every day. While the runners got ready, Rupantar made sure that everything was ready, and that the counters had arrived and had clipboards with lap sheets on their tables. At the same time he managed to record a short pre-start video that he uploaded later on to the official site. He showed the results board and said a few words on how things were at the race. He was good at adding a bit of humor to his comments. We had to observe the time, as at 3 minutes to 6 am Rupantar started to invite everybody to the starting line. He always did that with good humor, and had to invent new encouragements to get the runners to rise from their chairs and go to the starting line. Then we had a minute of meditation and there was the 'Go.' command.

The other directors of the race had no fewer

concerns. Bipin was a night guard at the camp. Sahishnu uploaded the results to the Internet, plus printed out the runners' mail twice a day. Every evening for 2-3 hours Sandhani rode his bicycle around the course, making sure that the female runners were safe in the late night hours. Each of the directors was on duty at the race for 4-5 hours daily. They solved all kinds of problems. If there was a need for a tent over the massage table, they saw to it. If a helper or a runner had a toothache, they told the directors. If we were out of ice, the directors brought it, packed it in baggies and even handed it out to the runners. They gave us ice cream and they laid the dinner on the table. How is it possible to do all that. They must have a minimum of four hands each – or, perhaps, one golden heart.

I also remember very well the love and concern that Bahula showed to the runners, especially the girls. She was responsible for medical help, so she found and coordinated massage therapists and other medical staff at the race, and she herself cared for us. Her experience at multiday races has helped her to solve practically any problem. Every morning she came 40 minutes after the start to participate in the singing group 'Enthusiasm Awakeners'. For half an hour they sang many cheerful and uplifting songs. It is their way of helping the race. After each session they offered some refreshments to the runners and their helpers.

After singing, Bahula inquired about the state of the runners' health, fetched medicine, gave advice and then went to her job at the UN.

Every morning 'Enthusiasm Awakeners' cheer the runners. Bahula is the fourth from the left

After work she came back to the race and helped the runners. After the day was over, she drove one of the girls home and then gave a massage to one of the girls who needed it. Quite a few times when coming out of the bathroom I was surprised to find Bahula already waiting for me. When she was massaging me, I fell asleep and was oblivious to what was going on. More than once I learned that Bahula had left at 2 am and the next morning was back on the course at 6:40 am. Her mild and constantly smiling eyes, her cheerful and sunny disposition regardless of any tiredness, and her kind heart, worked miracles. Even at the mere sight of Bahula I felt much better and happier. And her gifts, which she brought to the course at different times, could cheer you up.

Another woman who came to the course three times a week was Hilary. Her story astounded me. Almost all her life she had lived in Brooklyn, and once, visiting the Indian area of Queens, she went to a store where she met Dr. Kumar. The doctor practiced Ayurveda and often helped the members of the Sri Chinmoy Marathon Team. Doctor Kumar

is a wonderful doctor and a very special person. He emanates inconceivable energy – very mild and full of love. He sees beauty and perfection in all and everything around him. Hilary started visiting him from time to time, and once he told her that she should move to Jamaica Hills in Queens – exactly where the race is held. Soon she moved and got acquainted with a woman who was a member of the Sri Chinmoy Marathon Team (SCMT). On learning that Hilary practices massage, she invited her to help the female runners at the 3100 miles. Hilary agreed to that and started to come regularly. The touch of her magic hands helped a lot, and I always eagerly awaited those days. Saturday was a special day, as on that day, on the opposite side of the road, the SCMT 2-mile race was held, plus Bahula and Hilary came together, and the four-handed massage became a real feast for the body, although it lasted for only 15 minutes.

Once, Hilary came to us in the evening and first gave Nidhruvi a massage. I asked to shift the break to 7:45. The moment we entered the van a most powerful rain started. It was like a tropical downpour, very strong and short. I was lying down on the couch, laughing. In the afternoon when I had run with Nidhruvi, we discussed the evening forecast, and she said she hoped very much to be in the van at the peak of the rain. It turned out quite the contrary. When she got back on the course the downpour decided to show how strong it could be. In 20 minutes the storm began to subside, at the same time as I was to finish my break. Hopefully, I asked if the rain was going to stop in 5-10 minutes. If so, then I would prolong the blissful moments of the massage. But nobody knew for sure so I got out of the van with my big umbrella. It was the first time I had used it at the race. The umbrella was in the form of a cane and its canopy was as vast as heaven. A person could stay dry in the strongest rain. The only drawback was its weight. It was quite heavy and not at all easy to hold in gusts of wind. But that evening I was even glad to have an opportunity to train my arms a little. For a few weeks, since the start of the race, I had only been running and not exercising my arms, so they became very thin and all my arm muscles were practically gone.

One time, Hilary said that perhaps she had moved to this district only to find the course. Twice we ran together for half a lap or the whole circle, which I liked very much. I wanted to know more about a person who came three times a week without pay for her work, and who gave her time and energy to massage us – why? In one of our conversations she said, "I believe in kindness." For me that phrase became the key to open the door of my question.

During the entire race I had two of my best friends near me – Pati and Manjaree. They came from Russia only to be with me.

Manjaree always surprised me with her ability to give joy, lightness, and care. She managed to lead me out of any intricate psychological state, and on seeing her I was smiling and laughing by the next lap. It is very important for the helper not to plunge into the psychological predicaments of the runner, but to be able to snap them out of the 'loop' they get

into, to drive their attention to something else, to cheer them up. One time, late in the evening, there gathered a few helpers from Russia and the Ukraine. I could hear them singing Russian folk songs 100 meters from the camp. They sang them loudly and merrily on purpose. It so amused and cheered all the runners. But that was only the beginning of the party. Within a couple of laps the helpers started folk dancing. They remembered everything – the so-called lezghinka and the dance with a handkerchief, plus even dancing in a squatting position. I laughed so much that night. All the pain went in a minute. Laughing is the best medicine.

Manjaree and me

Everything was always easy with Manjaree. Her self-giving knew no limits. She could easily go to Manhattan (a half-day trip) only to fetch some bottles of milk from a specialty shop. Teekshanam, the runner from Switzerland, told us that the milk from that shop did not stimulate secretion of lactic acid that results in muscle fatigue. Manjaree bought the milk for both of us. Before going to sleep I drank that warm milk with a big spoonful of melted butter as a way to maintain my bodyweight.

One time at the race it was Manjaree's birthday. We had bought a present before the race, prepared some flowers and a birthday card. Then we waited for her, and when she came she looked so sunny and unbelievably happy.

The bouquet we presented to Manjaree was arranged by Pati, the creator of many more a bouquet at the race, as all kinds of occasions – my mom's arrival, at the finish, as a token of gratitude to other helpers, etc. – Pati has a wonderful sense of beauty. Our friendship was born many years before and it was due to Pati that my love of running manifested.

Smiling Pati, near the stars on the asphalt, which the helpers dedicated to the runners

Pati spent so many sleepless nights at my bed during the race. Each night, after another full day, she gave me a massage, and early in the morning of the following day she was re-applying some plaster tape to my toes. By my return in the evening there was a foot bath with salt ready. Her love and self-giving were boundless. I had always known that Pati herself dreamt of running that race, and inwardly she ran beside me, shoulder to shoulder. Such oneness is priceless, and it gives the runner tremendous strength.

I was also surprised and very much inspired by the hearty support shown by seasoned participants to newcomers. Passing by with the speed of the wind, Vasu from St. Petersburg always found the time to ask me about my state of health, and whether I needed some aid. Pranjal shared some oil for my feet in the days when I stepped on the concrete like a rooster skipping on a frying pan. Sopan also shared some ointments, drops, and advice. Stutisheel many times rescued me with proper medicine at the proper time, and cheered me up with funny jokes. Nidhruvi was always nearby with her advice for every predicament too. When she herself had difficult times I also wanted to support her as much I could, with a kind word, a smile or a joke. Sometimes we sang together, and sometimes we just ran in silence. Knowing that there was a heart and a pair of feet near you, having an experience close to your own, made things easier.

Running shoes

It is really fortunate to find a model of running shoes that answers all your needs in terms of design, quality of material, weight, pronation, provision of cushioning and degree of rigidity, and many more parameters, including your size.

For a couple of years now I've been favoring Brooks running shoes for the combination of good cushioning and lightness. Before that I had always been a fan of Asics, but because of the weight of the shoes I switched to Brooks. Before the race, Pati and I went to a store and found a few pairs of Brooks on sale, so we bought a few different models, some of which were new to me. If the body of the running shoe of a specific brand suits you, there is a good chance that many models of that company would fit you. In Russia, the choice of suitable running shoes is more limited, and the prices are much higher than those in America. That is why I bought all my equipment, especially the shoes, just prior to the race or during it.

The size of the shoes changes, I always start a race in shoes of my training size, then for one day I run in shoes one size bigger, and the rest of the time I use shoes two sizes up. It is normal for the feet to enlarge in multiday races. I knew that and was not at all surprised. When the race is over, it all normalizes within a week.

I had never cut my running shoes in the special way the multiday runners do, this time I also decided not to experiment. Despite the fact that almost all

of them ran with the trim cut out from the front part of the shoes, at first I ran as I had always done at multiday races, without these special cuts. It was hot the first few days – more than 30 degrees centigrade – so my feet began literally burn. I followed Vasu's example and cut the shoes like his: three holes about a square inch each, one in the centre of the vamp and two in the sides of the uppers. After a week or two of suffering from burning feet I decided to have the shoes cut to Stutisheel's fashionable design. That, in the combination with the new socks, helped a lot.

Of course, it was not me who cut the shoes – as a rule it was Manjaree. A brave helper, she became a real professional in turning a brand new pair of running shoes into a perforated one – also, she cut the holes into different shapes. She was excellent at it. Pati was a bit cautious of this big responsibility, but by the end of the race she, too, took the scissors and skillfully cut out all that was needed.

Besides the cuts in the shoes, we ripped off the foam rubber from the tongues and sewed them up again with the stitches on the outside, in order to avoid them rubbing my insteps. Many runners did the same with the heel counters of their shoes, to make them smaller and to avoid some of the pressure on the Achilles tendons. Some participants cut out the whole of the heel counter.

The styles of the cuts differed greatly with the runners – it was easy to know to whom a pair belonged, as all of the runners had their own intricate pattern of cuts. It was also possible to recognize the runners by the sounds with which they ran. It was our favorite game – to guess who was catching up with you. The easiest to identify was William, who had very short and frequent steps, it was his unique style. The next easy-to-identify runner was Stutisheel: you could hear his shuffle long before he passed. I could tell it was Stutisheel when he was running 15 meters behind me. I was not far from Stutisheel in shuffling, and Nidhruvi always teased me about it. But when I discovered for myself light running shoes with a thin sole, I started to run as lightly and silently as a Kenyan marathoner, although I definitely was not as fast.

My route to the running shoes with a thin sole was a long one. A few years previously in Moscow I tried the FiveFingers running shoes, but the memory of the experience is not a very pleasant one. That was why I decided not to try running shoes with thin soles. However, when we crossed 'the equator' and the race was in its second half, my legs were so tired that I felt uncomfortable in any of the shoes I had, so I had nothing to lose and began buying completely new and unknown models in the hope that something would do. Thus I purchased two pairs of Saucony and a new pair of Mizuno with thin soles. As a rule, I put on the running shoes with thin soles in the evening, when my legs felt any additional gram of weight, and at the same time I wholeheartedly wanted to run quickly and easily.

The running shoes that I was about to use were kept at the course in a huge plastic box under my table. That allowed me to change shoes at any moment – I did it at breaks when I felt that a particular pair was not comfortable enough to run in. The box always contained 6 pairs, of which 1-2 were brand new and the rest had already been used.

All the pairs were tied together with their shoelaces, as it was easy to mix them up. Many of them were the same models with the same colors. It was important to make sure the pairs were not mixed up, as the wear was different. And, of course, the right shoe and the left one must be worn out evenly, as it influences the placement of the feet. That was why we numbered the shoes, writing on their backs with a marker. On average, my shoes were worn out on the outside of the heel in 2-3 days. Over the 52 days I ran in 30 pairs of running shoes.

Box with shoes

Because Sarah from Australia ran without helpers, she had to make all the cuts on her running shoes herself. The primary pauses in her running were due to changing and remodeling her shoes. Some runners took scissors with them for a lap and managed to do everything on the go. I often thought about the runners without helpers and asked myself

– if they had helpers, would that speed them up? I also asked myself whether I would be able to run as they did, alone. In reality they were not alone, as everybody at the camp was one team, and the care and help of all the helpers spread to all the runners.

Insoles for the shoes are one more detail that can change a lot. During the race I ordered four pairs of insoles for cushioning; we called them 'the greens' because they were a green color. A change of insoles helps a lot with the 'burning' of the feet. Besides, they can cushion the impact of the feet on the concrete and correct the placement of the feet. There are a great variety of insoles – thick ones and thin ones, with gel, cooling, correcting the landing of the foot, etc. Many runners use a combination of insoles. For instance, in the evening when I put on some lighter shoes with thin soles, I inserted a double insole from my other shoes. The shoes with thin soles were better with two thin insoles than with a thick one. These sensations are very subjective and individual and the optimal solution is found by trying many different variations.

Moreover, I always inserted a heel pad – sometimes it was a gel one, sometimes one made of a firmer material. I put it under the insole and that helped to reduce pressure on the Achilles tendons, as with a raised heel the tendons stretched less. It clearly saved me from pain in the tendons. In spite of the fact that they were inflamed and I could not touch them, I was able to continue running and without pain. The heel pad helped to solve the problem.

One of the basic principles at multiday races

is not to concentrate on a problem but to look for a solution. It is worthwhile trying everything. Sometimes a solution can be quite an unexpected one, but a runner should not get upset over an injury, some pain, or the impossibility to run as planned. It is best not to expect anything but to look for solutions and not to lose heart at the emergence of unexpected circumstances.

Different types of correcting pads for insoles

Shoe repair

How many pairs of running shoes are necessary for a multiday race? At the 10-day race I used 1-2 pairs. But what happens to shoes when you run 50 days is difficult to predict: I found out that a mere multiplication of the two pairs in a 10-day race by 5 would be an inaccurate calculation. The weather is different at the 3100 and shoes rub more in the heat. Besides, at shorter multidays, there is less fatigue and it is easier to lift the feet, so there is less shuffling and less rubbing from the shoes. For me, the main reason to change shoes is the rubbing of the bottom of the soles in the heel area. Starting from day four I started to shuffle a lot.

I wore out 7 pairs in the first two weeks. Some shoes were still wearable, but they were worn on the outside of the heel some 5 mm, which meant the foot landed differently, and there was more chance of injury. Such a speedy and intense wasting of the shoes puzzled me: before the start I had bought 9 pairs, so it meant I had to buy more shoes urgently or think of something else.

The organizers told us the good news: that they could invite a specialist who produced and repaired shoes. He could repair the worn shoes by gluing some material onto the heels, thus making the soles even. I was very happy with this new opportunity and the next day I met the person who worked these miracles with shoes. In addition to taking the worn pairs, he said that he was ready to make some special pads to help get rid of any discomfort and pain in the feet. The offer sounded quite attractive. It was impossible to resist, so I immediately blurted out everything about the burning and swelling of my feet, and showed him what was giving me pain and where.

After taking my footprint, he said that he would

bring everything in two days. Indeed, in two days he came with the repaired shoes. At the worn out spots, he had cut off the soles and glued on some new material. He also brought some special pads, which were glued to the insoles. Then my arch had some support, and under the ball of my foot there was one more insert, preventing extra pressure at the front.

When we were looking for an exact position for the pads, the specialist noticed that I had very wide feet and that I should try extra-wide running shoes. I had wide feet? I could not believe my ears. I always knew that my feet were very narrow and often some shoes were too wide for me. In reply, he shook his head and pointed to the front of my feet. Now I really noticed that my feet had become unusually wide at the instep, but how was that possible? He answered that there was nothing surprising in that – my body was adapting to the strain, and feet that are wider in the front provide more balance and stability. I was amazed, but that really demonstrated how amazing the body is.

About three weeks after the finish, everything went back to normal; my feet resumed their usual parameters, both in length and width. Perhaps they realized that all the stress was behind them and now they could return to their usual state.

To be able to outsmart your own mind

Once, when the time for the evening break was approaching, my helper and I were discussing some organizational matters and trying to come to some agreement with other people. It was before my mom's visit. Normally communication between the runners and their helpers takes only a few seconds at the camp site, but solving these issues took me quite a while this time. When I thought of my evening break, the one I had not as yet taken, it was already 9 pm and there were only three more hours until the end of the day. Perhaps I could do without the evening rest and continue to run until midnight? I felt good: the main task was to persuade my mind that there was nothing awful about skipping the break once, that I was not tired and could easily run for three more hours. It was not such an easy task: the thoughts of possibly traumatizing my tired muscles, and the inability to run the next day, kept coming despite my efforts to ignore them. The idea of maybe having a rest was circling in my head... and that was in spite of the fact that physically I felt good and was not tired.

Then I decided to try something else – to imagine that I had just come out of my evening break, that my body was well rested and had the necessary energy for the remainder of the time. I had to really believe in it. And as soon as I did, all unnecessary thoughts ceased to bother me, plus I began to go faster. I felt a burst of energy as if I had really just finished my break. It was difficult to believe what

had happened. It is incredible to what extent our state really depends on our mental attitude and what we can believe in. That evening, in my savings box of miles, there were a few more laps, due to the power of imagination and faith.

In a few days I heard a similar story from another runner. He told me that once he had had no breaks at all for an entire day and felt wonderful at that.

Dipali

Dipali is the holder of the world record in the SCMT 6-day race. She comes from Australia and has lived most of her life in New York City, where she lives now. Almost every day she came to the course and ran in the opposite direction, so she saw all the runners each lap. She often came during the hardest and hottest period – around 1 pm – and stayed at the course an average of two hours. She is a very joyous and cheerful person. During her daily jogs she often joked, waved her hand to us and sometimes even made funny faces to cheer the runners up. When she was at the course, I had new strength. Sometimes we jokingly entertained each other. When it was hot I had some ice in my hands to cool me down, and on seeing Dipali I tossed it up and she would catch it. Once she ran up to me and started tickling me. I laughed and continued running, thinking up a joke during my next lap, to answer her back. So the laps flew by one after another quite unnoticed. In difficult moments Dipali always had some advice.

One night closer to the end of the race, I had very painful feet. No matter what shoes I put on, they were uncomfortable and rubbed my feet sore. After I told her, she had a plan of action by the next lap. Seeing me at the camp site she seated me on a chair, quickly took off my shoes and socks and started actively kneading my feet. At last I felt the blood circulation in my lower limbs – sometimes it seemed that while remaining in one position my feet grew numb and I could not feel my toes. By the end of the race it happened that something was interfering with my running and I bent to see what it was. I saw that I was stepping on my own clenched little toe. That evening Dipali massaged my feet, found some sheep's wool in the medical tent and put it between my toes and under the pads of my feet. What a relief it was. That piece of wool I used until the very end of the race. It prevented the rubbing of my skin against the socks and the shoes. That simple solution became real bliss for my feet.

The presence of this one person on the course changed something for me. I knew all that she said had been proven in practice a million times, and that she herself is a person of incredible willpower and childlikeness at the same time. When we were running the 6-day race and it had been raining for the second day in a row, we met on the course one night. It was very cold and I was chilled to the marrow from the low temperature and ceaseless rain. Trying to find a way not to give up, I started talking to Dipali, asking her the silliest questions,

only to keep up the conversation. Having asked about the weather forecast for the next few days and getting the reply I had already known – heavy showers for the next 24 hours – I was upset. In response, Dipali said that there was nothing wrong with the rain – children like to jump in puddles and spray themselves and everything around them, getting matchless joy from it. Remember that state. I remembered myself very vividly when I was seven. At that very moment everything changed – now I wanted to start jumping in all the puddles on my way. I saw that very rainstorm with different eyes. I felt so much joy from every drop and the entire world became different – bright and light – although everything around was the same as before. Just one of Dipali's phrases had changed the day for me.

That year Dipali set a new world record in the 6-day race. She was over fifty at the time and did what she had not been able to do at forty. She always tries to raise the bar to an ever-new height for herself, and age never stops her – by her will and her way of thinking she is able to transform her body.

The power of trees

During the race I was ready to use most unusual – sometimes seemingly amusing – means of recovery, of protection from injuries, and of energy support. Some grass in my shoes – yes of course; sandalwood powder on my skin – no problem; buckwheat sprouts to eat – with pleasure, and how was it possible to go to the course without a cabbage leaf in my socks? Sure, we often used psychological ways of escaping pain and injury: visualization of light in the painful spot, inwardly diving into the heart, where you can rise to a level of consciousness higher than the physical one. In this way it is possible to ignore the suffering of the body and to become one with the soul. And once, for some reason, I wanted to pick up a piece of bark from one of the huge trees growing along the course.

Those trees were more than 10-15 meters high, going up and up almost to the sky, and their circumference was so large that a person could not embrace them. They resembled age-old oak trees, only their leaves were in the shape of maples. I very much liked to run in the area where the trees grew on both sides of the sidewalk, and their tops bent to one another, making a beauteous arch. Thus the trees offered the runners some protection from the sun. Looking at them I felt the tremendous force hidden in those giants.

The day when I was ready to make every possible effort to get rid of the pain in my shin, I took in my hand a piece of bark from one of the trees. The trees had shed their bark and there were pieces

of different sizes on the sidewalk. Then I looked at those trees with new eyes, and it seemed to me that they emanated something magical. I felt that they possessed practically infinite power, only I had to feel it and believe it.

Soon, Yuri from the Ukraine was passing me, and for some reason I wanted to share that feeling with him – something told me that he would understand. As soon as I started to talk about the trees he nodded and said it was true that trees had incredible power, and that he had a story about it.

Once he had been swimming not far from the place where he lives in the Ukraine, when suddenly he heard a cry that resembled that of a child. Having come out of the water, he did not see anyone, but realized the cry was coming from a tree growing on the shore. Its trunk had been badly cut and the bark had been ripped off. Yuri felt how the tree was suffering and was asking for help. Without a second thought he collected some clay, mixed it with water and put the mixture on the cuts in the trunk. The cuts started to heal day by day, and Yuri often came to the spot to check on the tree. He told me that after that, he felt he had established some real friendship with that tree. Once during a 10-day race, in some difficult moment, he remembered that tree and started to invoke the tree inwardly to help him. After that, he felt that the tree asked the trees along the course to help him and the relief came. Yuri said he knew that all the trees were connected – they are one system – and then, whenever and wherever he asked them for help, the help always came.

Reading these lines I smile involuntarily – is it

really possible? But I believe and feel just as strongly that it is true indeed, and my experience shows that it is all reality itself.

With a piece of bark in my hand

Fatigue is forgotten

One day, when it was hot as the Sahara Desert, and the humidity resembled the subtropics, I had

little energy left. I was always amazed how the humidity influenced my state. A difference of just one number on the barometer can influence an entire day. How can this number take all your strength, so that it becomes impossible to control your own body and it simply ceases to listen to you? You do everything in the same way as the previous day, but have 20 % fewer laps. Your legs, it seems, are trying to show their full independence and separateness from the rest of your body – they completely refuse to obey.

On one such day, my friend Natasha, who was in New York at the time, came to the course. She joined me for a couple of circles and, apparently, I was not able to hide my rather broken state. Indeed, every lap was an ordeal for me, and my energy was evaporating somewhere. Natasha decided to support me and quite suddenly started to sing aloud a song from a movie from the Soviet Union times, about partisans, 'Uncatchable Avengers':

Fatigue is forgotten, and there's waving smoke,

And once again the hooves beat like a heart...

For me this song and the movie were always associated with something heroic and full of patriotism, dedication and unwavering aspiration to one's goal, and that mood was very much in tune with the race. Natasha and I sang that song a few times – we were able to remember only two verses, and the other words were escaping us. I was really uplifted by the song and in one moment everything changed: the heat was not so great anymore, and the humidity was not very noticeable. Now my mood was very determined – to move forward as soon as possible and without compromise. It worked. I really ran considerably faster, and no outer factors could stop me or slow me down.

That song stayed with me until the end of the race. I sang it quite a few times and was encouraged by it – a few times I even sang it out loud.

Singing. How wonderful that there is music in the world and we can sing.

The physical ups and downs

It turned out that the body could easily tune itself to a workload and adapt to any conditions. Before the race, the organizers had told us that a couple of weeks after the start, once the transition period is over, you would feel better – what was important was to find your pace, and to outlive the first weeks. Indeed, after the euphoria of the first days there came a time when the body needed to adapt to the unusual load, and I needed to find ways of solving many new problems – for example, burning feet. However, in a few weeks I realized that my muscles were not as tight as before, and received the same load more easily. The body got used to limited sleep and the regime of constant running.

The following weeks were even and stable, and my number of laps per day did not vary significantly. Once, Stutisheel asked me how I felt – to what day I could compare my state. After a bit of consideration I answered that I felt as if I were running only on the second day. It was truly so, although I could not understand that phenomenon. Behind me there was a month of running – a few thousand kilometers – yet the sensation in my legs was only better day by day. There came a new freshness and lightness, although a few weeks before it had been much worse. Stutisheel replied the same – his state was if not like on the first day, then like on the second. The mystery of the human body sometimes seems incomprehensible.

The last two weeks became physically difficult again, as the body began to feel run-down, though inwardly it was a very joyous time. With some runners it was different: as the race proceeded, their speed and stability only grew. William from Scotland was just such a phenomenon.

Friends amongst the locals

Among the locals there were a lot of people whom we saw every day – in the morning when they were going to work and in the evening when they were going home. I met many different people:

interesting ones, unusual, strange, amusing, abstracted, and friendly ones. With everybody who passed by the course, there was some special connection established – each of them got in touch with the race and some of them became a part of it. In New York City people are different, really different; sometimes it was interesting just to observe the pedestrians.

Every morning a man went to work on one side of the course. He always went to work barefoot, holding in one hand his brown leather briefcase and in the other his sandals. Perhaps he enjoyed going barefoot. It seemed to me he was always concentrated on his own thoughts, not looking around much. Once I saw him talking to one of the runners: every runner had their own relationship with people around them.

In the morning and in the evening there were adult exercise classes on the baseball field adjacent to the course. They were mostly attended by rather large women, but there was one athletic young man. The groups were coached by a young African American; he himself trained quite actively. He came to the sessions listening to music on his headphones – it looked like he never noticed what was going on around him. Some runners saw him as sullen, reticent and self-absorbed. But for some reason he often waved to me. He never asked me anything and we never talked, but I always felt some benevolence and support. It is amazing that such a trifle as a wave of a hand or a 'Hi' may mean so much.

It always caused me to smile inwardly, and the smile persisted for a few laps, plus it gave me an inflow of new energy.

I very much liked to watch this training on the field. I saw determination and eagerness – it was obvious that most of the women wanted to slim down and be fit. They moved to that objective persistently and determinedly; the exercises were not easy for most of them. The training sessions were very varied, but in the middle, they all had a task to run a circle or two on the race course. As a rule, they ran in the direction opposite to us, yet one time they ran in the same direction. It was a real shock to me. Right in front of me a large woman ran, and mostly she did not even jog but walked. However, no matter how hard I tried to catch up with her, I could not do it, and she always remained ahead of me, quite unreachable. By the end of the lap it was so funny to me that all my efforts to at least get nearer to my new running friend were futile, that I laughed aloud – and still was not able to catch up with her.

I felt a powerful oneness with these people – a month and a half of silent communion. We saw each other a few times a week and observed the desperate struggle of everybody to improve, each one persistently and purposefully moving towards their goals. In a way our goals were similar: we all wanted to change for the better.

On the day of my finish, their training was in the center of the field, so it was difficult to shout to them and I was not able to share my joyous news. But after the finish I ran the additional 15 laps to complete 5000 km – that was when I gave them a cheery wave and they waved back. Then I shouted to them that I had just finished. In reply, I heard loud congratulations and a question – why was I still running? I laughed and said that the distance was done, but I wanted to complete 5000 km. They laughed again and I laughed, too.

There was one more local who came to the race course every morning when we were getting ready for the start. As early as 5:45 am, he passed through the camp and greeted everyone. He was originally from Bangladesh. Those who had run the race in previous years remembered him well. Sometimes he came a bit later, and often during his morning walk he gazed only in front of him and looked very concentrated. He did not pay attention to anyone – it seemed he was praying or doing some other spiritual practice. Then, having walked a few circles, he changed completely and started saying 'Hi.' to all the runners. For some reason he smiled very rarely – oftentimes he just greeted us.

Once in the middle of the race he walked his 7-10 circles as usual, facing us. We had already greeted each other, but suddenly for the first time I saw him running the next lap. He ran in his flip-flops, ironed trousers and shirt – he was always dressed like that. He ran for the first time, in all those days. He was so happy that he even waved to us and a smile was shining on his face: so he was running for two laps. When I saw his sparkling eyes, glowing face and smile, I wanted to jump to the skies. It gave me so much enthusiasm, and immediately I thought that

perhaps that is how the world changes – very simply and unnoticeably, becoming better, being filled with good vibrations and joy.

Perhaps just seeing that somebody is doing something good, a passer-by may be inspired and also do something good, thus a chain of goodness will continue and embrace the entire world. What is important is to start with oneself.

A few times when I was running on the course, a car stopped and the occupants said or asked something about the race, and it was clear that they had seen people running there before. It did not surprise them anymore and they asked for news from the course. Once, a sports car stopped and a young man asked in a very friendly manner, "How much is left?" I told him how long we had been running and how many days were ahead. He wished me luck, waved his hand and drove away.

Another day, a large jeep stopped by the route and a young man – perhaps a Hindu – folded his hands prayerfully, bowed and said, "Thank you for doing this." He did not ask anything, he just thanked us and left. It touched me very deeply: his words and gesture were very simple but had incredible sincerity in them. Passing by that spot, I remembered the episode many a time.

Also, very often a man by the name of Chris came to the course. He was black, very tall and large, with a clean-shaven head. He always smiled and brought some coconut water to the course. He made sure to greet everybody on the course with the firm gesture 'fist to fist', like some teenagers do in American movies.

Such simple signs, greetings and smiles introduced a wonderful feeling of unity with people, a feeling of warmth. When you spend the entire day alone with yourself, these signs become a million times more important.

Among the locals there are many friends of the race. During its 18-year history, almost all the locals have learned about it. They are no longer surprised to see people running in the morning when they go to work, during their lunch break or even in the evening when they return home from work and go out for a walk with their children. Many of them brought watermelons, pies, and the local community of Hindus brought a fruit salad once a week, usually slightly sour from the pineapples. Even now when I am writing these lines I vividly remember the taste of that fruit salad.

One day, when I was running on the part of the course that goes along the service road, Stutisheel was running in front of me. I noticed how a car stopped by him, and the passengers started to wave to him and he waved back, then the car was gone. Later I found out that the family in the car used to live not far from the course, and they had often walked their two big dogs there. The family became friends with some of the runners – it had all started about ten years previously, when their son had been little. Now they live in another place, and their son

is quite big, but the tradition to support the runners remains. In a few weeks, when Stutisheel finished, they came again especially for his finish. One of the dogs had died and the other one had become old, but those people still came to the course with pleasure. A lot had changed in those ten years, but Stutisheel ran as before, and the family came to support him as before. Perhaps it was a real friendship and a unity of hearts – you may see each other only a few times a year but always remember each other.

To trust

When I took part in the 6 and 10-day races, I met a chiropractor, Mitch, who gladly came to all our long races in New York and helped the runners. He himself loves running. I met him many years ago while I was running my second 10-day race. Having had a lot of experience working with multiday runners, Mitch can easily determine the cause of a pain and quickly fix it with a few skillful movements.

Once, during the 10-day race, when I was on his couch undergoing treatment, one of the twists was not very successful and my inguinal ligament was strained. It would remind me of its existence for a few years during long races. That is why, this time, when I learned that he was going to be one of the practitioners at the 3100, I was not sure if I would go to the treatments very often.

During his first visit to the 3100, he saw all the runners who wanted to go to him. Vasu insistently advised me to go to Mitch, but I was not in a hurry to do that; then Nidhruvi asked me if I had been to him. I was of an opinion that if nothing bothered me, then I would not go to a practitioner, but would continue to run. That day I thought I felt good enough to continue running without a chiropractic adjustment. One of the reasons I was not in a hurry to see practitioners was my desire to economize on every minute and not to lose time. But he saw me when I was running by the massage table and invited me to come up with a gesture of his hand.

The visit was quite short, no more than 5 minutes, and oh, miracle – I really felt better when I ran on. Despite the fact that I did not have any serious injuries at that moment, after that express adjustment, it was even easier to run. Then I thought that the most important thing was to trust, and not to rummage in my old memories of what had been a few years ago. The past is dust, and every day we can start by erasing past disappointments.

After that, almost every time Mitch came to the course, I tried to use the opportunity, and in a few cases he really reduced a considerable portion of the pain with one movement. Miracles did happen. When your pelvis is put in the right position, the pain might leave your knee or ankle at once, as the load is distributed more evenly and correctly. Mitch's express treatment indeed worked miracles, but the most important thing was to believe and trust.

Morning laughter

When running is all you do for the entire day, you have an incredible amount of time, and it is good if you have an interesting subject for reflection. One example of what to think about and how to occupy the endless time was to think of some sketches to perform. Some runners rehearsed them on the go and then performed them for the 'Enthusiasm Awakeners', the singers who sang cheerful songs every morning for the runners. It all looked very simple – the plot to be staged was a joke or a real-life story from the course. Then two or three runners performed that joke for a minute or two. The girls from the singing group were the main spectators of such a mini-theatre. They always laughed merrily in the end, even if the joke was not the best.

I always adored the days when I took part in those little sketches, and a couple of times I told the joke alone because there were no other girls around, or simply because the idea came to me so suddenly I did not have time to invite anybody to participate. Those morning performances gave laughter, joy and merriment both to the spectators and to the actors. Following is a story of such a performance:

One morning I was running with a glass full of grapes. I had already eaten most of them, and during each step the berries jumped in the glass. At one point they got packed together. They stopped jumping and were tightly pressed against each other – I could even turn the glass over and they stayed there. Such a spontaneous trick I demonstrated to the 'Enthusiasm Awakeners' singers and just in case,

I had pressed the grapes some more beforehand. So I became a magician for the first time in my life. So many things happened for the first time at that race. Little discoveries in life, even small ones, give so much joy and apparently they can be found every day.

Stutisheel and Sopan while performing

Suprabha at the course

Suprabha is a unique woman from Washington, DC – she has finished the 3100-mile race thirteen times in a row, not missing a year and spending

all thirteen summers at this course. Never in my life had I seen a more simple and modest woman, literally glowing from the inside. When I was near her, I always had a feeling that I was standing near a saint. But Suprabha herself obviously did not think that. She often smiled and joked, and was always in good cheer. Indeed, without such qualities one would not run far in this race.

That year she was there at the start of the race, and later on she came a few more times. Her little presents to the runners were always right on time – she brought some baby food as puree and juices, and many other necessary or simply pleasant things.

One of her helpers, Bhagirathi from New York, came to the course almost daily, and once she told us that in the years when Suprabha had run, the race was organized much more simply – there were only 4-5 runners, and the food was limited in variety and even in quantity. Usually local restaurants that wanted to aid the race provided three hot meals per day, and the rest was brought by friends of the race who lived nearby.

When I heard that story I could hardly imagine it: now the runners have all kinds of dishes, from freshly squeezed juices and berries – bilberries for instance – to hot meals from the menu of a vegetarian restaurant, or you can pass on all your wishes and preferences to the incredible team of cooks at the race. There is a team who not only do their work most professionally and deliciously, but also self-givingly. In short, there is everything needed for running. We only had to think of running – how simple.

But let us return to Suprabha, as it is to her this chapter is dedicated. I loved it when she came to the course, then we were able to run a couple of circles together. The counters jokingly told her the number of her laps as if she were running the race again. She laughed merrily and continued to run.

Suprabha came to the course to support the runners

Once, when we were running on the side with a lot of traffic (the service road next to Grand Central Parkway), I asked her about her attitude towards the passing cars. She answered that the noise always reminded her of the ocean, and it is the ocean that she imagined while running on the side with the traffic. That image was so unexpected and at the same time so obvious. Closing my eyes and withdrawing my focus from the road nearby, I could also clearly hear the sound of the waves. When a car approached, it seemed that a wave ran over a sandy shore, and the noise of distant cars created the

sounds of the far-off ocean. The sounds were very similar indeed, but not everyone would notice the similarity – only the one who wholeheartedly loved the race could think of such a comparison.

Your own style and pace

Each runner had their own style of running, and their own pace. I noticed a few particular features.

Some runners moved with a permanently steady speed during the day, they had a minimum of breaks, and ran continuously all the remaining time – not very quickly but steadily. In short, they assiduously moved towards their own goal, step by step. Pranjal was in that category. I was from the ranks of such runners too. We preferred the strategy 'slowly but steadily' – a strict discipline, an even pace, a meticulous observation of time, and limited scheduled breaks. Nidhruvi and Yuri were also closer to that type.

The others ran quite spontaneously. When a flow came they flew faster than the wind. If the flow did not come then it was time to have a little break and a good stretch, to get ready for the time when the flow would come: to be in excellent form, to be able to answer with willingness, to become a speedy river and rush with it full speed to the limitless ocean.

Some runners moved at medium speed during the day, but in the evening they rushed at full speed, resembling my pace in a 10 km competition. They flew faster than the wind. It could go on for about 5 hours and during that time they were totally concentrated. Sometimes they listened to music, not allowing any thought to enter. It was important not to think of anything in those hours and on no account to allow even a hint of a thought that from such fast running an injury is possible. It is important to feel the flow and give yourself to it entirely.

It turned out not to be a simple task at all – many times I noticed how I was thinking consciously or unconsciously that to run fast on tired legs was a sure way to get injured. It was difficult for me to fully exclude such thoughts. But a few times when I was able to do that, I got in a state where the running was fast, easy and completely safe. However, I felt that for myself I preferred a permanent, regular and steady pace.

What definitely united practically all the runners was the lack of thoughts about tomorrow, following the principle of complete self-giving to every day. Pranjal said that in the evening, climbing upstairs to his room on the second floor, he was on his knees because he could not walk up. And if he could climb the stairs on his feet, that meant he had not given everything.

All the runners tried to give everything every day and not to think of the future. Then magically during the night there came a new energy, and the morning gave the strength for one more day.

Hindu in an orange dhoti

Running is a real meditation: rhythmical breathing and repeated movements help the mind leave its endless flow of thoughts. The inner space begins to exist only for the depth of a silent ocean inside and for the heart's joy. Then the running turns into a movement without effort, the light flow carries me like a bird, and the endless sky becomes my friend. This lightness and joy are enough to bring me happiness, and I do not need anything else. But once, I wanted something more, and offered an inner prayer for a spiritual experience which I could not only feel, but also see – which would be as tangible as the trunks of the trees I passed while running, and that I could always touch.

There was broad daylight and the sun was generously giving its rays to everybody on earth. On one of the laps, I saw a man in an orange dhoti far away. He was approaching me in his bright garment. I was at the part of the course that goes downhill and he was ascending. It was so unusual that in the beginning I could not even understand who the man was and how he had appeared there. In the multinational borough of Queens one could meet representatives of any country, but it was the first time I had seen a man in an orange dhoti.

He was of medium height with sandals on his bare feet. When he walked, his hands were moving freely in sync with his light gait. His movements were very natural, and resembled those of a young Sri Chinmoy in one of the films where he was walking through green fields in a light-crimson dhoti. When he came alongside me, he folded his hands in a prayerful gesture and bowed slightly, and I did the same. It seemed that the meeting took place not on this earth but in some magical world – there was something mysterious in it. The image of this man stayed in my memory, and for some reason remained in my heart.

Pain in my knee

One day, when I could not remember how many days I had been running but I knew it was still a long way to the finish, at midday when the sun was at its zenith but the break was still a few hours away, suddenly I felt a pang in my knee. It came where I had never felt it before – on the outside of the upper part of the knee. The pain was so acute that I had no choice except to walk. I tried to massage the knee myself, which worked – the pain went away – but after a lap it returned.

After a few attempts of self-massage I decided to switch to walking. Soon Nidhruvi came alongside me, and seeing me walking, she inquired what had happened. Having learnt where I felt the pang, she literally cried out that it had been exactly the reason why she had to walk for three days the previous year. Needless to say, 'inspiring' news. Nidhruvi advised

me not to get upset, as I had some miles in store and could afford a day with low mileage.

To be frank it was not at all inspiring, but I had no choice, I had to accept this new experience. To my surprise I managed to remain in emotional balance. I continued walking, trying not to be upset by this new occurrence. I was focused on my feelings, on my breath, and I felt that I was ready to accept everything I had to go through. Stutisheel stopped by and in reply to my story about the pain he said that he had something to help. He gave my helper some ligament recovery tablets. I was to take three tablets every 3-4 hours, and so I did, continuing to walk. To my surprise, in an hour and a half, it seemed to me that the pain was almost gone. I could not believe it, how was it possible? Perhaps it only seemed so? Could such an acute pain come and go in an hour and a half? There was only one choice – try to run. At first I tried to jog slowly for half a lap, then switched to my normal pace, and oh miracle. I could run again.

What was that: the wonderful effect of the tablets, my thought power or a hallucination? I decided to take the tablets for a few more days, just in case. I had to order them, so I went to an online shop and read the description of those tablets – it turned out they were for liver pain. The indication for use did not say a word about knees, ligaments, tendons or joints. I laughed so much upon learning that some liver pill had cured my knee. Maybe there was a magical connection between the liver and the knees or, possibly, the power of thought and faith could work miracles.

Vitamins

During extreme effort, the body needs some support, especially during multiday adventures. From the very beginning I decided that I would try to use natural preparations. I became acquainted with a representative of a company producing biologically active additives, and purchased a few preparations to test them. To be honest, I did not feel any effect whatsoever, but I thought that since I was able to train so much, to endure so many hours of strain, it was a good enough sign. So I decided to use those preparations at the race. They were extracts of different herbs that had some amusing names: Dandelion, St John's Wort, etc. I increased my intake to three times the recommended the dosage and took them twice a day. During the race the biggest strain is on the kidneys, liver and heart, therefore I chose the preparations that support the systems of the body influenced by these organs.

I also took some vitamins and microelements:

- Vitamin C – one gram 2-3 times per day and more often when injured.

- Trace Mineral drops – a complex of minerals 2-3 times per day, added to water with some lemon or orange juice.

- Calcium and magnesium – 2 tablets twice a day (300 mg).

- Magnesium – twice a day (200 mg), help to relax the muscles.

- Heat Guard salt tablets – one tablet 4 times

per day.

- Water with salt, honey and lemon.

- Kefir or probiotics – 1-2 times per day.

- Spirulina – twice a day.

- Protein cocktail – once a day.

- Honey products (ambrosia, royal jelly, honey with propolis, or bee glue) – in the morning, in the afternoon, and before going to bed.

- Dried magnolia-vine berries – 2-3 berries during the day, for strength and energy.

When taking so many supplements, you never know what works and what does not – the list and the dosage are subject to some inner feeling, experience and logic. Amongst the runners there were those who did not take anything at all – with the exception, perhaps, of isotonic drinks. As for me, the intake of those supplements was important; even psychologically it gave me confidence that I was supplying my body with what it needed. It is possible that next time I will reconsider my vitamin plan. I may take it easier, having understood that the source of real strength is not in the food and supplies.

Alternative medicine helps

Alternative medicine is widely used at the race. Ayurvedic medicines are among the most commonly used. Often these are creams, powders, herbs and sprays – natural and very effective. Twice I resorted to one more type of alternative medicine – acupuncture. During the race nobody paid much attention to tight muscles, as it was a natural reaction of the body. Some days it was more, some less, but even with tight muscles it was possible to run. Despite that, once during the race my left calf became so rigid that it started to worry me. The Achilles tendon also became stiff and painful. Hilary practiced acupuncture as well as massage, and offered to try it on me. I thought about it for some time, as I had never tried it before, and decided to go for it. We started with three needles to see how my body would react, and to my surprise it worked quite quickly – as early as the next day I felt the effect. My calf started to relax gradually and it was much easier for me to run. Later we were also able to relax the back surface of my hip.

One more unusual method was Chinese cups. The principle is the same as with the customary cupping glasses our parents applied in our childhood. When the cups suction the skin there is increased blood and lymph circulation, which aids the quicker healing of inflammation. At crucial points when my shin was on the verge of being inflamed or was already in its initial stage, we applied the Chinese magnetic cups. They were plastic rounded cones with some magnetic elements inside. The air was

sucked out with the help of a special little hose and pistol. The entire procedure took about 10-15 minutes.

Variations of cups

There was one more version of the cups — rubber ones. Some runners even tried to run with them, which looked very funny. The cups became an express method for eliminating pain in the Achilles tendons and the shin. It is a simple and effective method worth trying and having in one's arsenal.

Miss stability

In the middle of the race, the number of my laps was quite predictable. It stayed within 108-111 laps per day, and I still had some energy to push harder if

I was not making it. I could shorten my break and as a result run the needed 109 laps. Only twice I left the course before midnight – once when I had an injury and the second time when I ran 110 laps by 11:30. Then I decided to give myself a rest, and at midnight I was in bed already – what bliss it was. I tried to repeat that many times, but the cherished 109 laps emerged only by midnight.

One day, when I had completed 109 or 110 laps again by midnight, Sahishnu, one of the race directors, called me 'Miss Stability'. We both laughed. Later at the finish he also said that I was one of three participants whose results for all the days had three figures, i.e. 100+ laps.

Every evening after coming home, the first thing I did was to mark the number of my laps on the chart over my bed, plus my balance for the day, i.e. the difference between the actual and the required laps. I had one more line for totaling up the extra laps. Thus every evening I knew exactly how many laps I had in reserve. During the first half of the race I accumulated over 50 laps and that cushion helped me a lot during the last two weeks of the race, when the extra laps started to gradually disappear.

Every night when I got in Sandhani's car, I told him how many extra laps I had in hand or, conversely, had borrowed from my account. That was our ritual, and I looked forward to sharing my joy with him when I had added a lap or two. If that night I had to subtract some laps from my balance, Sandhani always told me not to worry, that I would have many good days. One evening during the last two weeks, when I was short of some laps, he told

me that I would definitely have more fast and easy days. I could hardly believe it. It seemed that speed was nowhere to be found and yet two days later I ran two extra laps – fantastic.

Crying

Once somebody asked me how often I cried during the race. To answer this question correctly is impossible – it took place innumerable times. The tears were completely different, but I loved all their sides and manifestations. After tears had streamed down my cheeks I felt much better.

Among the brightest and unforgettable were my tears of joy during the finish ceremonies. I will never forget the finishes of Yuri and Vasu. When they held in their hands the race banner and their countries' flags, their eyes shone with light, beauty and the kindness of their hearts, reflecting gratitude for that long and rich journey, and happiness at the unforgettable moment of the finish. They stood right in front of us, but looking at their faces I felt that in that moment they were in quite a different world – the world of the soul's light – and they were uplifting everybody lucky enough to witness that historic moment. In those minutes the tears involuntarily streamed down my cheeks and I felt a profound oneness with the finishers.

Vasu's finish

Looking intensely at their happy faces I could see no trace of tiredness, and in my mind's eye I saw dozens of pictures – as if from a family album – of the way they had run to reach that finish.

All I could see in those 50 days was only an outer manifestation. What really happened inside their dauntless hearts was known only to them. But the love and care they poured out to everyone during the entire race moved me to tears, so I cried some more without embarrassment, and those tears gave me tremendous joy.

Yuri's finish

Once, Utpal – a member of the organising team, who every day published incredible articles about events at the race – interviewed me. The day happened to be Nelson Mandela's birthday. Utpal asked me what I thought of the man and whether I could compare myself with him. I would not dream of comparing myself to such a great person – each of us plays our own especially predefined role. Continuing our conversation, I began to talk about the equality of people, of one prayer that every runner carried inside – a prayer for world peace, for mutual respect, love and appreciation between people, and for not killing one another. Saying those words I began to cry unexpectedly. At that moment I wanted only one thing – peace on earth. It was my soul's cry that overpowered everything else. For me at that moment there was only a prayer for peace. I asked myself why the world had wars, and prayed

146

for the oneness of the entire world.

Other kinds of tears I had every morning when my body was completely stiff, when I was slowly going downstairs at our house and every step was unbelievably hard. I had no idea how I would run in 10 minutes. When we lined up at the starting line, I tried to hold back my tears, but very often after the start I could not hold them back during the first lap. I shed tears, never trying to stop them. I cried earnestly and loudly. Only when I heard someone approaching me, I would keep myself under control for a few seconds. The crying lasted a lap or two or three, and then I felt unbelievably relieved. I started to laugh at myself and I could hardly believe what had gone on a lap before. By the fourth circle I had warmed up, the teardrops on my T-shirt had dried up, the singing group had come to the course and life again gave smiles, laughter, and joy at every step.

A bandage on my hip

Even before the beginning of the race I had sprained the back of my left thigh. I wrapped an elastic bandage around it from the very start of the race – it was much easier to run that way and the hip almost did not bother me. For balance, I sometimes

did the same with my right hip. At first I was embarrassed to run with the bandaged leg because it made people worry and ask me what was wrong. In a few days I got used to it and the questions did not embarrass me anymore. A few times I tried to run without the bandage, but by midday the pain in the leg had increased, which led to my right leg having to compensate for the weakness of the left one. And that in turn could lead to an injury in my right leg. As I resigned myself to bandaging my thigh every morning, it became a rather quick procedure, and even the pattern became quite an artistic one like a neatly braided plait. Week followed week and closer to the end of the race Kausal – a doctor from Italy came. He traditionally visited the race to help the runners cope with their recent injuries. The profile of Kaushal's practice is very wide. His methods include healing with herbs, oils, homeopathic preparations and chiropractic. He feels the source of a problem very subtly, and precisely finds the best way to deal with it.

At one point he asked me why I was wearing the bandage on my thigh. I told him my story and explained that the bandage was a great help. He smiled and said that I did not need it anymore. It sounded incredibly persuasive and left no room for doubt – I took it off at once without asking unnecessary questions. I was confident that if he had said I did not need the bandage it really was so, and I continued to run as if I had never had the bandage on my leg. By that time I ceased to be surprised at the wonders taking place on the course. I never needed that bandage again.

Friends

Almost every day I talked on the phone with my friends from Moscow and Kiev, and with my mom. All that took place while I was running. I put on my headphones and ran with the telephone in my hands. I so wanted those conversations to continue longer. During the communication with my dear ones I took no notice of the laps passing by, and the running became incredibly easy and imperceptible. Such conversations usually took half an hour or even longer, and I managed to run 3-4 laps.

In addition, I knew that during the race a few nice surprises awaited me: my friends would be visiting me on the course. At the beginning of the second half of the race my friend from Moscow was coming – Ludmila Popova, my swimming coach. I eagerly waited for her arrival, and I also knew that her arrival would mean the first part of the race was over. Ludmila was to arrive in the fifth week of the race. For me it was a significant event that I had been waiting for. During our conversations by phone we often discussed the moment of our meeting on the other side of the globe. Ludmila and I had been preparing for a year for two important events: she was going to swim the English Channel and I was preparing for this race. Interestingly, both the distances are called 'Everest' – one in swimming and the other in running. It turned out that considerably more people have climbed Mount Everest than those having swum the English Channel or having run the 3100.

One evening when it was raining heavily, at

last the event we had been discussing so much by phone took place – passing the camp I saw the smile of those familiar eyes. We hugged each other right there in the rain and started laughing – perhaps because of the incredibility of all that was going on. She flew halfway around the world to support me when it was needed, and later I would be on the boat during her swim.

All week Luda trained in the ocean during the day and in the evening she helped me on the course. She also helped Pati to massage me before sleep.

**The helpers' team – how good it is
to have dear ones beside you**

During that week Luda made friends with all the runners and helpers. At her departure nobody believed she had been at the course for only six days – it seemed she had been with us for ages. We often laughed with Luda; she always knew how to amuse and cheer me up. I did not want her to go, but I knew that pretty soon there would be a dearer person with me, or even the dearest one – in a week my mom would arrive. It was about 10 days before the finish and we had been preparing for both the visits.

Pati made a beautiful bouquet of flowers for my mom's arrival, and Bahula volunteered to meet her at the airport. I still see my mother's happy face when she could give me a hug and make sure I was really well. Right away we ran a couple of laps to share at least some of the news. Mom had already helped me in 4 multidays (6 and 10 days) but there she noticed everything was different. A shorter circuit made a helper's work harder, as they had to do everything twice as fast, and I needed quite different things for the breaks. There were many fine details, but as my mom wanted to help at least half of the time, she soon adjusted to it. The first night when we returned home from the race she nearly jumped at seeing my feet – what on earth had happened to them? Sure, my feet looked a bit different than usual but to me they seemed to be in excellent shape: just 5-6 blisters fixed with tape, and some peeling skin – not that bad. I had no nasty deep blisters, and no black or lost nails. My mom heroically got used to my feet and even learned how to tape the blisters on my toes.

All the runners were glad when my mother came to the course, and it seemed she became a mother for all of them in those two weeks. They all called her simply 'mom' while talking to her, and she tried to look after not only me, but also everybody else she could possibly help.

The energy of silence

I was lucky that during the race a few of my friends were in New York. Often, especially in the morning before going to work and in the evening after work, they came and ran a couple of laps with me. It gave me a lot of support. On seeing my friends from a distance I was ready to jump to the sky – so much energy and joy they gave me. We ran together while I told them the news from the course and they shared their news.

In the middle of the race I felt that it was getting more difficult for me to communicate, especially in the evening. Although my heart was still happy at the sight of a familiar smile, I could not run with anyone anymore. I felt that even a simple conversation cost extra energy. I could not be distracted by the things they told me, and even more, neither could I tell them about the events on the course. I needed complete concentration on running. I dared to tell my friends that I would rather run alone in the evening, as it would save energy for running.

Once they told me that late in the evening, when it was already getting dark on the course and the beautiful halo of the moon was visible in the sky, they were passing by the course in their car. They drove in the same direction as we ran. Coming alongside me they slowed down and started signaling and shouting, trying to draw my attention, but in vain. I did not hear a thing and was not able to notice my friends five meters away from me. It was a great surprise to hear this story the next morning, because I had not heard any voices from the road.

The last two weeks my communication with those around me became increasingly laconic and brief – to a great extent it was reduced to communication through eyes, smiles, gestures, and only when necessary, through words. It happened naturally. I noticed it only after some time and then I understood that my entire system was rearranging to save energy. I was never an advocate of unnecessary talkativeness; I would prefer a mood of silence. But what happened on the course became an interesting confirmation of the notion that conversations require extra energy. The only difference is that it is not easily noticeable in our daily life.

Scottish power of concentration

William Sichel from Scotland became the first runner over the age of 60 to finish. He did not look sideways. His gaze was always directed a few meters before him, whatever happened. Later, he said that all the time he had been concentrating on his breath, repeating inwardly the word 'breath'. He also imagined a ball of energy in his abdomen area, and with every step he inflated the ball, thus getting some strength for the next step, and the next lap.

The race developed in different ways for William.

At first, as with every other runner who challenges the race for the first time, he had difficulty finding his own rhythm for the race – all the more so, as he had no helper in the first two weeks. Moreover, the weather in a New York summer differs greatly from the coolness of the faraway Scottish island where he lives.

But on the very day when his helper arrived and they both worked out an optimal schedule, William practically flew. He was determined, and that determination found its outer expression in his stable and fast running. He managed not only to catch up with the required mileage, but also to finish a day prior to the deadline.

With his helper they found means of adapting to the heat: equipment in the form of sleeves was of some help, then a broad-brimmed hat, and of course some ice in his drinks and under the hat or cap, plus his favorite ice cream – around a kilo of it per day. The finish of the race for that not-at-all tall, skinny and ever so strong Scotsman, was one of the most moving ones. William was shining with happiness and everyone around him was doubly happy. Before crossing the finish line he stopped right in front of the finishing tape and held high two flags – the flag of his country and the flag of the race. He even shouted something. Seeing him stand at the finish line I rewound in my mind's eye the pictures of the superhuman efforts he exerted daily to get to that line.

During the award ceremony they sang a song about Scotland, and his eyes were wet with tears – perhaps he himself did not believe what had just happened. The last weeks he was helped by his true friend, who had assisted him at dozens of races – even at his first 24-hour race, when he had taken his first steps into the world of ultra distances.

During his 3100 miles William set some 20 records, including world, national, and age group ones. He finished late at night when it was already dark, and the lights decorating the finish zone gave special warmth to everything. Everybody who came to see his finish was treated to ice cream.

William at the finish line

Ray

Ray, a high school teacher, was the only participant from the USA, and he happened to be quite a remarkable person. Ray had known about the race for a long time. Once Sri Chinmoy told him personally that he would run the race and that he would feel when the time would be right. Years passed. At age 59, Ray realized that the time had come – he must run, and if he did not appear at the starting line this time, the moment may never come. He drove 500 kilometers in an old car and arrived the night before the start. He just made it to the ceremonial moment of the start when we heard the long-awaited 'Go'.' command. He arrived during the introduction of the participants with a big camera on his neck, just in time to take a picture of everybody, and with a playful smile he joined the runners.

Ray is the liveliest and most spontaneous child of all the adults I know. While running he imagines himself to be a flying airplane and imitates the sound of the propeller. He sings songs loudly – he loves being the center of attention and indeed deserves it. Ray continuously composes songs while running. They turn out to be very funny, moving, and they rhyme quite beautifully. Here follows approximately what I could hear while running near him in the morning: "I woke up today and saw it's the most beautiful day, as I see this colorful world every day and it is marvellous as never before. She has run past me again, and her eyes' smile always lives in my heart. Why do you run so fast? I want to sing you my melodious tune."

Ray has run a countless number of ultra-races, and in his younger years he was very fast – even now he covers some 160 km in a 24-hour race. He always has his phone in his hands and from time to time he takes out his camera. Ray made friends with all the passers-by: he had no problem talking to a woman passing by, to teenagers sitting on the bench, to a girl swinging on a swing. He always had a topic for conversation, talking about our race with great enthusiasm, and he would always smile with his fascinatingly kind eyes that reflect love for the entire world. He competed in a rap battle with some guys going to school, and they practically jumped to the sky when hearing some of his phrases, shouting, "Cool."

One day in the middle of the race I saw Ray running with unbelievable speed almost nonstop, only shouting to Sahishnu to please pour him a drink, and then again disappearing beyond the horizon. I did not know then what was going on and only wondered what had happened that made a usually-walking-runner Ray turn into a sonic-speed-rocket. Sound was always accompanying his appearance. I just heard something about his T-shirt he had on that day. Only after the finish I learned the full story.

It turned out that on the same day about 20 years before, Ray was taking part in an ultra race. He took off his T-shirt and threw it in the direction of his table, but the T-shirt fell on the ground. Sri Chinmoy was walking nearby at the time and he picked up the T-shirt. That was how they first met and in that unusual manner their conversation started. They

were two very different people, but close in spirit – with their ability to rejoice and to value every moment in life, to see the beauty of everything around them and to remain a child at any age.

Since then Ray had always kept and taken care of that T-shirt. In remembrance of that historical meeting with Sri Chinmoy, Ray put on his T-shirt the same day many years later. Ray wanted to make that day of the race special, and so it was. Later, Ray said that he had felt some special force, and it had not let him stop. Even in the moments when he wanted to rest, something inside made him continue running. Thus he spent all that day on his feet and covered more than 65 miles. That day he had a real fire in his eyes, and even from afar we felt his unusual state – it seemed that he was charged with a great flow of energy and that he had to spend it all.

I remember one more day that started like dozens of other days. Nidhruvi and I ran again together for a few laps and, running past Ray, we heard the merry tune of his song and the lyrics describing what he saw around. At that moment we were ahead of him, so evidently he saw us, and Nidhruvi and I became the subject of his song. We ran a bit faster and he kept our pace to sing the song. In reply Nidhruvi and I composed a few lines, and so started some merry composing of songs and verses. Ray continued to run with us, and when Nidhruvi and I switched to walking at the camp site, Ray took a cup of water and continued to run without losing pace. He has a marvellous capacity to keep a stable speed and not to waste a single second when he is in a flow. At any moment he could easily stop and have a half-hour conversation with some college professor, but when he got into his special flow he did not lose a moment, and started moving with lightning speed. So, having flown past us, Ray started to gain his cosmic speed and again rushed into some unearthly flow. That day Ray and I ran the same number of laps – 111 – and on hearing that our mileage for the day was even, we gave each other a high five as bosom friends.

Last days of the race

Starting from day 44, the runners began to finish one by one. It was accomplished with joyous ceremonies, moving words, tearful eyes and matchless emotions.

It also meant that the next morning there was one less runner at the starting line.

All the runners revealed through the race their own special qualities and the character inherent in them. Thus there formed a certain aura at the course, with its own energy.

When the participants began to finish I noticed that the atmosphere was still maintained wonderfully. The qualities particular to the finisher expanded to the other runners. And even despite the fact that a runner was not at the course anymore, the common feeling at the race was kept

intact. For instance, after the faster runner's finish I felt that their speed was transferred to the other runners, and some of the participants began to run considerably faster than before. After Yuri and Vasu finished, their cordiality and care were still at the course, as if redistributed amongst the rest of the participants. It continued for a few days. I observed that wonderful feeling and was amazed how it was possible.

The atmosphere of the race can be felt in the faces and eyes of the runners. Left to right: Ananda-Lahari and Stutisheel

Closer to the end, during the last days when there remained fewer of us and only 7-8 people stood at the start, I had a feeling that we missed the others very much, and it seemed that with their absence something was lost. Fortunately, all of them without exception came to the race every day and always ran a few laps, sharing the light of their happy and rested eyes, the shining smiles of finishers, with those still continuing to run and dreaming of waking up without the sound of their alarm-clocks.

160

The last day there were seven of us – half the number at the start – and it seemed to me there were so few of us. That day, I recalled that at the first races 18 to 19 years before there had been only 5 to 6 participants, including only one lady. One could run half a day then without meeting any other runner. When runners had a pretty similar pace they could run without seeing one another for the entire day, communicating and supporting each other only through their helpers.

At times it was the way Nidhruvi and I communicated – through our helpers – and it was so amusing.

The relativity of time

Duration of time is very relative: sometimes an hour lasts for eternity, and sometimes days fly by in a moment. I asked myself many times: what is the secret of this riddle?

In the middle of the race I began to consider the notion of a week equating to a day back home. That 'day' was not too short, but neither was it too long – one weekend was followed by another. Weekends were not similar to weekdays, so I took Saturdays as a reference point for counting weeks. When there were only two weeks left, I did not think that it was

much in comparison with the time that had already passed. I continued to run as usual, focusing on the current day, current lap, and current step. Thus the second to last week passed unnoticeably. But when the final seven days did come, I felt it was only a little time, and the finish was literally around the corner.

It turned out that a week could last as long as a month. Pranjal had told me four days prior to his finish that the last 3 to 4 days was one of the most difficult periods of the race, because the finish seemed so near and a runner's concentration shifted from the present moment to the future. Thoughts came about what would happen in three days – here days –how the finish would be, and what would happen after. And all those thoughts meant the point of attention was not in the here and now. The mind got into gear and started functioning much stronger than the heart.

Being in the present moment, I felt the fragrance of the morning air, the aroma of freshly cut grass, the movement of a light breeze, and followed my own feelings – I dived into my heart and not into a ceaseless current of thoughts. It was similar to the easy and pleasant going with the flow, when time became unnoticeable.

During the last days the thoughts of the finish did come. There were moments of counting the days and hours, estimating what time I could finish, and I even checked online the results of previous finishes with times close to mine. But all that did not give me any joy. Then a moment came when I realized that I would like to be not in tomorrow's finish, but on the lap I was running right now, and it again gave me the feeling of flight – of going with the flow, even if the outer speed of that flight was not very high.

The day of the finish

On the third of August, when I heard my alarm clock as usual at 5:10 am, I immediately smiled. That morning I did not feel sleepy – on the contrary, I wanted to jump out of bed (or, rather, due to my physical condition at the time, to crawl out), and to be on the course as soon as possible. I knew that it was the last day I would be on the starting line of the race that year. There were two reasons for that: firstly, I hoped to finish that day, and secondly, it was the last day of the race. Even if I did not complete the whole 3100 miles that day, the next day I would not find the vans or the results board, or the food table at the start camp. That day was really the last day of the race.

I got up, put on my favorite shorts with my favorite orange T-shirt, went downstairs and waited for the car. I sat on the bench near the house, breathing in the freshness of the morning air and enjoying the sight of the rising sun. Everything around seemed perfect – the grass with drops of dew, the blue sky with floating clouds, the houses around, looking alike but still with their own

character, and predominantly my feeling of myself was unbelievably light, peaceful and harmonious. Dissolving in those feelings I noticed that the car had already arrived. With some difficulty, as on all of the 50 previous days, I went down the steps leading to the pavement, crossed the lawn and got into Rupantar's car. After a pause when no words were needed, the car started and Rupantar almost immediately said that I had to be especially concentrated today. I wondered why, as the finish was so close and it seemed nothing would interfere with that. But I did not ask about it and simply thanked him. We picked up Nidhruvi, and she congratulated me with sincere joy: today was the big day for me. I replied that it was the big day for all of us.

Soon we arrived at the course and within a few minutes we were asked to line up at the starting line. It was 5:55, I stood a bit ahead of everybody else, and there was a flower garland on my neck. It was the tradition that a finisher was given a flower garland. That morning I had one made of lilac orchids.

There was no anxiety inside, only joy and the feeling that everything was as it should be, plus gratitude, as I knew that it was due not to my efforts, training or physical capacity, but due to Grace, that somebody above or inside me had created such a vision and had chosen me for the manifestation of that vision. It was an incredible feeling.

Start on day of finish

A few hours prior to the finish they started to prepare the celebration. I was asked what colors I would like to see on the decorations. At the finish area they often tied ribbons to the wire fence in the national colors of the finisher's country – it was one element of the decorations. I wanted something sunny, so they made a sun with a yellow balloon in the centre and spreading rays, which all created a joyous, bright and shining mood.

At noon, Manjaree, Pati and I thought that it would be great to take a picture of all my running shoes and me. We collected 30 pairs. They were neatly arranged on three levels, and I stopped for a few seconds for our joint photo.

***Me, Pati, Manjaree, and a countless
number of shoes***

The last hours before the finish were full of preparations for the finishing ceremony: we ordered soft drinks, mangoes and balloons for everybody present on the course. There were many details, and all that distracted me a little from my state of inner absorption, but simple joy and lightness were always there. I marvelled how quickly the laps flew by that day. I realized that I did not want to hear the counter calling out the ever-increasing number of laps. It meant that the race would soon be over.

An hour before the finish, I noticed that people were coming to the course, and I understood that all of them would stay to see my finish. It was very moving – I had not imagined so many would come especially for that. Among the spectators at the finish were even the passers-by and the locals who had often greeted the runners. They followed the news, and always knew who was going to finish and when.

Before the last lap my mother gave me a new T-shirt with the emblem of the race. I changed my clothes and then Manjaree gave me two flags – the flag of Russia and the flag of the race.

How many times I had imagined that moment. But then everything was happening in reality. I held the flags high above my head and felt proud that I was carrying them – I also felt the significance of that moment. My head seemed to swim a bit with all the emotions, but it was a pleasant feeling. At last I saw the finish tape held by my mom and Pati. The bells were ringing and I heard a great many admiring voices, and in a few moments the finish already became history. I crossed the finish line of the longest race in the world. It seemed that for the rest of the day I was transferred from my usual world to quite a different dimension.

I stopped by the board with the results. The race songs, which had been composed by Sri Chinmoy, were sung by a group of singers as part of the finishing ceremony. I already knew all these songs by heart and started to sing along. That helped to calm my pre-finish excitement. The lines of the songs carried me with their flow to the world of the heart. I looked at the sky with its few clouds and at the faces around me, which all expressed sincere joy, and I even saw tears in some eyes. But I did not feel like crying at my finish at all. I continued to stay in the euphoria of some unearthly dimension. In those moments the whole world was inundated with light; it shone and was perfect.

Then Sahishnu read out all the statistics of my

running. It turned out that I was the fifth and the youngest lady finisher in the 18-year history of the race, and one of three persons that year to total more than 100 laps every single day. I had 32nd place amongst the 34 people who had ever finished the race. My time was 51 days, 12 hours, 31 minutes. I received a lot of flowers and then I was invited to say a few words.

Congratulations from my mom

Of course, those were words of sincere gratitude. I mentioned that my dream had waited for its fulfillment for 10 years. I tried to thank all the people who had been near me, and who had supported me all that time – with words, smiles, songs, running and advice. They were all my helpers: the organizers, the singing group and, of course, my mom and all my friends, and those who cheered for me thousands of miles away, who sent me their good will, their kind words and love.

For some reason I forgot to thank the team of

cooks, so now I would like to use the opportunity and say that the team managed in their inconceivable way to give energy to all 14 runners through their magical food, in which we felt their care and love. It is a true riddle how they were able to cook fresh and tasty food, taking into account the preferences of everybody, plus in such quantities, – 14 people had been eating all that time. Perhaps they themselves would not be able to answer this question, just as the runners would not be able to say how it is possible to run all that time.

The awards ceremony was coming to an end and I continued receiving congratulations. In reply I could only smile. Everybody took home a balloon that day – I so wanted for everyone to feel joy, and balloons always give me joy – plus there were some refreshments, and a huge, unbelievably delicious cake prepared by the cooks. But I still had 15 more laps ahead.

Only all together were we able to get to the finish

Those 15 laps could be run by all finishers wishing to complete 5000 km. More often than not the runners do it, but far from every time. I wanted to be alone with myself and once more to feel the joy of running on this circle. Hence without putting it off I ran those last laps. I ran in complete silence – I wanted to absorb the energy of this circle, to memorize the rhythm of my heartbeat, the feeling of a moment when my heart was wide open. I wanted to touch every tree and every leaf of the bushes, a latch on the fence, to be able to absorb the fragrance of the air, so that the infinite blue sky with white clouds would also stay inside me for good.

There was a time when I had asked myself why the runners returned to that circle. What beckoned them? And it seemed that I felt the same – I did not want the race to stop, and I wanted to continue running. A piece of my heart would forever stay on this course, regardless of whether or not I would be able to return here....

Ahead there was the final ceremony for those continuing to run up until midnight on the 52nd day. They were not able to complete all 3100 miles this time, but it is not for the round number that runners come to this race, it is the experience that is truly valuable and this is what beckons all of us. They continued to run until the very end and did all they could. Their eyes shone with unearthly light and the ceremony was especially moving. Each received a cake with a candle. As it took place at midnight, the candlelight gave some special coloring and beauty.

I did not set my alarm clock for the next day – I

knew I had earned a good rest – but my body woke me up at about 7 am on its own. It seemed that I had got used to little sleep and felt quite comfortable with this schedule. There was no need for sportswear that morning, so I put on some different clothes, but I was glad to go out for some fresh morning air and I shouted to the whole world that I loved it.

When I reach the top, I cannot stop
And I do not stop
Because I clearly see
A new goal beckoning me.

- Sri Chinmoy[4]

LIFE AFTER THE FULFILLMENT OF A DREAM

Having arrived in Moscow, I came out of the customs area and saw a large team with posters, flowers and toys. They were my colleagues and friends. My eyes filled with tears but we soon started to laugh, to hug and to take pictures. This greeting was quite unexpected for me and very joyous.

The next day I went to work already. Some amazing feelings were waiting for me: I was at the same workplace, surrounded by the same people, but it seemed that everything was happening differently – I felt myself to be a different person. I did not know what exactly had changed, but I vividly sensed I had become another person in a way, and

---

4   Sri Chinmoy, My Morning Soul-Body Prayers, part 8, Agni Press, 1999

because of that, everything around was changed too.

I have heard many times that after achieving a cherished dream, people are not able to find a new goal and they feel lost. I did not expect anything specific from my long-awaited finish; it was, rather, one more intermediate step. After climbing it one can see a new horizon and even sit for a moment and have a rest, enjoying a picturesque vista, as the height is really impressive. However, there are so many peaks and heights ahead, and I am still only at the beginning of the journey. It seems to me that I do not even imagine how high the highest step of the staircase can be. I like the following utterance:

Recovery after the race

The first six months after the end of the race there was not a single day when I would not return in my thoughts to those wonderful, magical, fascinating 52 days of my life, pulling me like a magnet. The first month I dreamt that I was still running. Those were very joyous dreams about the race – I even waited for them, and upon waking I always felt a smile on my face that at least in my dream I could be at the course and could run. In reality I was not able to run

for 8 months. When I got out of bed, for a long time my first steps were accompanied by pain, and even by tears sometimes. Often I asked myself if I would ever be able to walk without pain and to run again. But not once did I experience even one thought of regret.

It turned out that the race begins long before the start and ends much later than the moment when the finish line and the cherished 3100 miles are behind you. It is not for nothing that the race is called 'Self-Transcendence'.

Self-transcendence continued even when I got back to Moscow. Just as it had been earlier, out on the course, I was not going to give in to injuries or to lose heart. After some time I managed to cope psychologically with the absence of so customary a part of my life – running. There was always faith within me – if it was destined that I appeared at the start, I would be shown the way forward and all the injuries would go, as they could not be eternal.

During the rehabilitation period I tried various means of recovery, including physical exercises, self-massage, physiotherapy, hydrotherapy, acupuncture, Chinese herbs, salt baths, ginger applications, and paraffin and ozocerite applications. I tried to fix my feet, or to do light workouts, used kinesiology tapes, and applied shock-wave therapy.

I realized that these 8 months were a new period for me, and I had to switch my attention from training to something else, as everything in this world happens for the best. Nevertheless, to understand it was one thing, and to accept it with your whole heart was another: not always easy.

Only afterwards I realized all that I learned during this recovery period could not be received by me in any other time: I would hardly find time, desire or motivation to address issues of recovery, of developing strength and elasticity of ligaments and flexibility of joints, of working out and searching for new systems of training.

Here I would like to mention a few simple means of self-dependent recovery, which I found and liked.

1. Self-massage with the aid of rollers, balls, and etc.

This is a good way of improving your blood circulation in different zones. Different sizes of rollers and balls allow you to get to any part of your body. A good blood and lymph circulation means lessening of soreness in muscles, a faster recovery and healing of injuries, and better elasticity of muscles. Good circulation also gives a feeling of lightness and well-being.

I used a big roller and started to massage my calves by rolling along the muscles. In the painful spots I stopped for a deeper and more prolonged impact or did a few perpendicular movements, and after that 4-5 more movements along the muscles. Thus I went from one area to another, going up from the periphery to the central parts.

I rolled my calves on the back and on the sides; the hips were rolled on the back, the sides and the front. Then I went to the gluteal muscles and my back – I liked to roll on the upper part of my back, placing my nape on the end of the roll and moving gently to the back of my head.

I often used the balls at work – they were always under my table. This was a simple way to maintain good circulation in my feet, to limber them up and improve their mobility. A golf ball proved to be the best for a deep limbering of the feet, and I used two tennis balls tied in a sock for massaging the muscles along the spine.

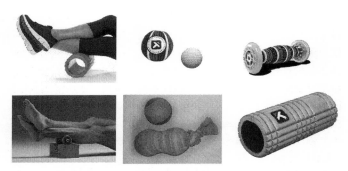

Examples of equipment for self-massage

Later I discovered for myself applicators and rollers with little spikes, which do a similar job to the above-mentioned means.

Applicator as an excellent way of recovery

I especially liked the spiked roller – its impact gave a very pleasant sensation of tingling, warmth, and a feeling of moving energy.

2. Temperature influence.

I learned this method from the long jump Olympic champion Tatyana Lebedeva. She healed her Achilles tendons in this way, and I also decided to try it.

When you put your feet alternately in cold and hot water, the blood circulation becomes very intense, thus making healing and recovery faster. In one bucket pour the coldest possible water with ice, and in another one, hot water. Keep some additional ice and boiling water nearby – I used two pails. You start the procedure by putting your feet into the hot water for a minute, and then you put them in the cold water for a minute. Repeat this 4-5 times, finishing with hot water. When necessary, add some ice or boiling water to maintain the difference between temperatures. After a week of such procedures, once or twice per day, you feel a considerable effect – the Achilles tendons recover very well.

I think the accumulated effect of all the therapies, my keen desire to recover, plus time – which certainly also heals – all together played their role. In a few months I felt that I could try to give some exercise to my legs, gradually involving my feet.

The first step was a swimming pool: I went aqua-jogging. You put some special equipment on your ankles – a kind of foam plastic that helps you to stay buoyant in a vertical position, as well as adding some load.

At first it was difficult for me to run even 100 m in the pool – I got tired. With time I was able to go for a few hundred meters, then I began to include some limbering up exercises for the flexibility of my joints, and even some accelerations. It was like a proper workout. On average it lasted 50 minutes, including the warm-up, plus dry land exercises. After such workouts I felt I had given my all. The movements in the pool were much more difficult than on land: the water resistance was not to be compared with that of air, and in two weeks of training, my muscles became considerably fitter. I was glad as a child when I ran for the first time in the swimming pool. Plus I did my favorite backward turns and tried out all the equipment for water aerobics. That training was filled with joy and fun, it did not create any expectations or frustrations – I felt good in the water. I did not need to swim enormous training distances; I simply did what gave me joy.

Later I started to add cycling, beginning with 15 minutes on an exercise bicycle. The fact that I started to train – although not in running – helped me a lot. Returning in my mind to that period, I understand that I was able to train again only when I had accepted that training at the time was beyond my capacities. But life was not empty or less full, it just became different.

At some point in the recovery I ceased to feel that life was incomplete without running training. Life went on and was no less beautiful. I understood that I had to wait calmly throughout that period. Probably it often happens like this – as soon as we are able to let our attachments go, all our long-cherished dreams come to us by themselves. What is important is to be open to all possibilities, including new ones.

Eight months after the finish, one fine day, I felt I could go out and try to run. The feeling came spontaneously and with confidence. I put on my running kit and went out. After a light warm-up I tried to run without any pain. I started with a few hundred meters on a soft surface and gradually moved to a kilometer, then three, and in a month's time I even dared to run 5 km in a competition. My time was 22:15, about 5 minutes slower than it had been a year before, but then it was such an achievement – like climbing Everest. It was a competition where I did not try to outrun anyone; it was as if I was taking my first steps. It is like with a toddler whose speed is not that important for the parents; rather, the very ability to walk is of importance. Now I could run, too. The medal from the finish of that competition is one of the most precious for me.

The end that is only a beginning

Before the start I had often thought that should I be able to run the 3100 mile race even once, my life would not have been lived for nothing: that one race would fulfill the mission of my soul in this lifetime. Nevertheless, when I stood at the finish, I clearly felt that I would be there again and would try to run the race once more. I do not know when or if this moment will come. But I will train again, and I will wait... I will wait for a sign that gives me the feeling that the time is right once more.

For now I would like to learn how to live every day as I did at the race – with the feeling of an infinite divine power inside me. I want to continue running in my life as I did at the race – to the rhythm of my heart, following the voice of my soul.

The race has shown, as vividly as ever, that inside me there is a source of ceaseless energy and strength. In extreme conditions the very soul gives a hint on how to find this strength and how to get to that source. Having felt and having experienced it once, it becomes much easier to find a way to it again. Now the new goal is really ambitious – to be in union with this source through every movement, act, breath, and in every thought. This goal is so eagerly awaited and indeed worthwhile to run towards, no matter how long the journey may be.

Jayasalini Olga Abramovskikh

Running in rhythm with the heart

A book on the love of running, and the dream to cross the finish
line of the longest race in the world – the 3100 Mile Race.

Additional information on web:
loveofsports.org
3100.srichinmoyraces.org
srichinmoycentre.org

Translation from Russian: Alexey Beysov
Editors: Sarita Earp, Sumangali Morhall
Design: Konstantin Schekotov
Photo credits: Utpal Marshall, Prabhakar Street, Jowan Gauthier

Made in the USA
Monee, IL
18 October 2023

44791209R10106